SCHOOL LIBRARY MEDIA SERIES

Edited by Diane de Cordova Biesel

1. *Chalk Talk Stories,* written and illustrated by Arden Druce, 1993.
2. *Toddler Storytime Programs,* by Diane Briggs, 1993.
3. *Alphabet: A Handbook of ABC Books and Book Extensions for the Elementary Classroom, second edition,* by Patricia L. Roberts, 1994.
4. *Cultural Cobblestones: Teaching Cultural Diversity,* by Lynda Miller, Theresa Steinlage, and Mike Printz, 1994.

Cultural Cobblestones

Teaching Cultural Diversity

Lynda Miller
Theresa Steinlage
Mike Printz

School Library Media Series, No. 4

The Scarecrow Press, Inc.
Metuchen, N.J., & London
1994

British Library Cataloguing-in-Publication data available

Library of Congress Cataloging-in-Publication Data

Miller, Lynda.
    Cultural cobblestones : teaching cultural diversity / Lynda
Miller, Theresa Steinlage, Mike Printz.
       p.   cm. — (School library media series ; no. 4)
    Includes bibliographical references and index.
    ISBN 0-8108-2966-5
    1. Multiculturalism—Study and teaching—Activity programs—
United States. 2. High school students—United States—Books and
reading. 3. Libraries and teachers—United States. I. Steinlage,
Theresa. II. Printz, Mike. III. Title. IV. Series.
LC1099.3.M557   1994
370.19'6'0973—dc20   94-37699

Contents

Introduction
Creating Cultural Cobblestones

Life

Life on Earth
Growth and form take
place
Origin of the races
Forests and seas
People and places
Genetic engineering
The great chain of life
The living world

Jennifer Somers

Stacey Nodolf, Pen and Ink

Introduction and Purpose

For over thirty years I have served as a school librarian and have begun to develop a series of beliefs that I have about this profession. I'd like to take credit for this philosophy, but I must be truthful and acknowledge those students, teachers, administrators, authors, publishers, parents and a network of professional colleagues all over the country who have given input to this credo. One of the important ingredients in this philosophy is, I believe librarians, school and public together, need to let young adults know that we do not live alone on this continent or in this world. In 1988 Hazel Rochman, an assistant editor of "Books for Youth," *Booklist*, compiled a book describing what it is like to live under Apartheid (properly pronounced a-part-hate) in Southern Africa. She collected these autobiographical and fictional vignettes by South African writers when she was a school librarian and worked with a social studies teacher, Rita Headrick at the University of Chicago Laboratory Schools. I have always taken pride in the fact that I stay aware of current issues, but was appalled at how little I knew about Apartheid and the ghastly conditions in South Africa until I read Hazel Rochman's book, *Somehow Tenderness Survives*. I began to think that if my knowledge had been so minimal, what about the typical high school student? An informal survey in a Senior English class of thirty students showed that about one-half had very little knowledge about Apartheid and the remaining one-half had heard the term. Thus began a multicultural journey that would begin to change lives, attitudes and levels of awareness for students in one high school in the Midwest.

It is the purpose of this introduction to demonstrate the role of the school librarian in organizing multicultural learning experiences that begins with a library-sponsored Ethnic Week based on literature that stretches across the curriculum and the school year. Once that seed is planted, it is the role of the teacher to implement the ideas started by the library exposure. Thus, the purpose of this book is to show how two creative, innovative teachers expanded and enhanced the multicultural involvement that originated from the Ethnic Week sponsored by the school library. Lynda Miller's emphasis will concentrate on the visual arts and Theresa Steinlage's will focus on the language arts. The introduction will pay attention to other areas of the curriculum.

Diane Goheen and I are co-librarians at Topeka West High School and since 1989 we have promoted Ethnic Week, the first week in March, as the starting point for a multicultural awareness program centered around a single idea that reaches out across the curriculum. It is based on one book and extends beyond the designated week. Listed below are the Ethnic Week Programs for the first four years:

1989—Apartheid in Southern Africa
1990—The Holocaust
1991—The Native American
1992—The Hmong

It is the purpose of these Ethnic Week observances to raise the awareness of the students and staff members concerning a central theme. After a great deal of input, the library staff selects this central topic and thus sets in motion the organization of the week and faculty members plan how to embellish and augment the ideas and themes in their classrooms. Some functions of organizing the week are similar each year; others are specific to the theme.

When organizing such a week, the library staff members begin early in the fall selecting a theme. Books basic to the week's focus are carefully perused and one title is selected to serve as the basis for the multicultural experience. Each year the school's principal, Dr. Robert McFrazier, is approached and the librarians present their ideas for the program. His approval brings the money needed to support such a week, but his commitment and dedication underscore the impetus needed to make the week a powerful learning experience for the students and the faculty.

Fifty copies of the selected title are ordered early so that teachers who wish to participate can plan to have their students read the book, participate in discussions, and complete other readings before the week itself arrives. When the books arrive they are quickly processed and sent to scheduled classes. Because Ethnic Week features library forums, exhibits, a film festival, and a speaker's bureau, students need to complete the reading, take part in discussions and prepare three written questions to ask at one of the library-sponsored events. The success of the week is dependent on the fact that students have some knowledge of the topic before they participate. A 3-x-5 card with the three questions is a ticket to attend one of the said events. Spanning four years, instructors in the following departments have been involved in the Ethnic Week projects: art, foreign language, home economics, language arts, mathematics, music, science, and social studies.

Librarians design the following ventures for Ethnic Week.

1. **Library Forums** feature prominent speakers who are authorities concerning the particular theme. These forums are available to teachers who wish to schedule their classes to hear the speaker and make the commitment to have their students complete the readings, discussions and questions. These speakers make similar presentations in the library four to five times during the day and up to six classes with enrollments of 30-35 students can participate in one forum. In a typical day approximately 900 students may take part. The library forums will not be expanded to full all-school assemblies so the library maintains ownership. Library staff members prepare packets of 30-35 quality readings for teachers to use before classes attend.

2. **Exhibits** include student art work and written student compositions based upon the reading of the book selected for the year's theme. Econo-Clad Book Company provides books for an exhibit near the library's entrance.

3. A **Film Festival** features films and videos from the school district's central collection. Video stores have been willing to lend additional films for the week free of charge. Teachers receive a festival schedule several weeks in advance so that they can schedule the films through the library's audiovisual department.

4. The **Speakers Bureau** includes local authorities and knowledgeable school officials who have information to share concerning the topic. Forensics and acting students join this bureau to showcase their dramatic interpretations or monologues developed from the book selected to represent the current theme. A list of these speakers is made available several weeks before Ethnic Week and teachers select and schedule with one of the library staff members.

Student coordinators are selected from the student librarians and they help with scheduling, arranging motel reservations for speakers (some are free in lieu of a contribution to the school), selecting other students to greet and introduce guest speakers, arranging for sessions to be video-taped and run errands. These students write announcements for each day's activities and then read them over the public address system during the reading of the daily bulletin.

Much of the success of Ethnic Week depends on faculty support. Our administration occasionally schedules "planning period" faculty meetings to allow staff members to meet in smaller groups. One of these meetings is a month prior to Ethnic Week and the librarians are given an opportunity to speak at each session and create enthusiasm for the experience. Teachers also receive several memos concerning the activities. Samples of these have been compiled and are located in the appendix of this book. Some specific information about each of the Ethnic Weeks sponsored by our library might be useful and practical for others planning similar multicultural adventures.

The title for the Ethnic Week dealing with Apartheid in South Africa was "Somehow Tenderness Survives." The book used as the basis of the week's activities was:

Rochman, Hazel. 1988. *Somehow Tenderness Survives: Stories of Southern Africa*. New York: HarperCollins.

Library forum speakers included Prexy Nesbitt, Executive Director, Chicago Committee for Solidarity in South Africa and Rob Jones, Projects Director, American Committee on Africa, New York. Mr. Nesbitt captivated students and staff members as he gave a brief overview of a country that abounds in natural beauty, but has a social and political system that obliterates all natural wonders. He spoke of the other side of Apartheid when the South African government tries to extend the Apartheid system into bordering countries like Mozambique and Nambia. Students learned that there is an average of one death each eight hours in the mines of South Africa. They also were informed that by the presence of U. S. companies such as Goodyear, Holiday Inn, Mobil Oil and Coca Cola in South Africa, we are giving our tacit approval to the Apartheid system. In each of the standing-room-only library forums, students were given the opportunity to pose questions. These were insightful and searching questions which really showed the students' hunger for information on the topic. The situation repeated itself the next day when Rob Jones made an entirely different presentation. Mr. Jones brought a rap video on Southern Africa, which quickly captured the student's attention. He, too, was able to provide insight and interest among the students. As one teacher said at the end of one of the library forums, "I didn't know whether to get down on my knees and pray or buy a gun." Over 2,000 students filled the library to hear these speakers during nine forum sessions. International Foods students researched black South African culture and found recipes. One, an unusual nut cookie, was prepared and served to all students who attended library forums during Ethnic Week. Over 2,000 cookies were made and served by these students. Incidentally, the home economics teacher had her students complete readings, prepare questions and participate in the library forums. Long after Mr. Nesbitt and Mr. Jones had been taken to the Kansas City International Airport by a parent volunteer we continued to get positive comments.

Although the calendar week scheduled for the study of South Africa and Apartheid ended, the study continued. Senior English classes used the subject as the basis for persuasive papers; current events students wrote term papers. Using traditional library resources coupled with online searching on Dialog students produced papers with a depth and sensitivity not routinely found in high school compositions. Junior English students were assigned term papers on social activism and activists. Several chose to explore such personalities and topics as Nelson and Winnie Mandela, Steve Biko, Desmond Tutu and divestiture. The library was inundated with students who chose Apartheid and related topics as subjects for persuasive and informative speeches. The power of the book has been demonstrated throughout history. In one school, in one community, lives were changed because Hazel Rochman decided to compile the stories she knew.

The impact of the first Ethnic Week has continued for four years. Because of recent happenings in Southern Africa and the growing concern about racism in the United States, one- or two-day library forums have been made available. In late 1989 African artist Malangatana Ngwenya, of Mozambique, talked about the political strife and Apartheid in his country. With this internationally renowned artist, art and English students completed a mural based on their feelings after reading Hazel Rochman's *Somehow Tenderness Survives*. For this one-day event, the instrumental music department got involved. Their instructor had his students complete readings and discussions about Apartheid and then learn a song native to Mozambique. As Malangatana entered the library, the full school band greeted him with this number. He responded by joining them and did a lively dance as they played. In 1991, Prexy Nesbitt returned from Chicago to discuss South Africa after Mandela's return and to talk about growing racism in this country. In 1992, on the eve of the Rodney King verdict, Hazel Rochman discussed social and political situations in South Africa in 1992 and recalled what it was like to grow to maturity in South Africa as a white young adult. Shrouded in privilege and a supposedly liberal outlook, Ms. Rochman never saw herself as biased during her childhood in South Africa. Rochman told our students

> Apartheid didn't seem to have much to do with me. I grew up in a liberal home. I wasn't allowed to make racist remarks. I thought I was a good person. I didn't see what was going on around me. I took it all for granted. Never noticed that there were no black

kids in my neighborhood; not one black student in my school. I just accepted that the woman who cooked and cleaned for us and lived in a room in the backyard—we referred to her as the "girl"—I never thought that her children lived far away and she was forced to leave them in order to come and look after me. I remember vaguely that one of her children died. I never asked her about her life. Read a story about her? From her point of view? What point of View? Being white in South Africa was to be immensely privileged and blind. I didn't see. I didn't know. That's how you live with yourself in a corrupt world. You dehumanize the people and say they couldn't be as complex as me and think they don't feel like me.

Because of her husband's political activism and her own voracious appetite for reading, Hazel Rochman's eyes were opened to the reality of Apartheid. She has a new title that features truly unique multicultural bibliographies and booktalks.

Rochman, Hazel. 1992. *Against Borders: Promoting Books For a Multicultural World. Booklist,* American Library Association.

The central focus for the 1990 multicultural study was the Holocaust and World War II. The book selected as the basis for these activities was

Nomberg-Przytyk, Sara. 1985. *Auschwitz: True Tales from a Grotesque Land.* Chapel Hill: The University of North Carolina Press.

Library forum speakers included Holocaust survivors, a former Army intelligence officer, a rabbi and two Dachau liberators. The survivors can be located in many communities and should be video-taped so their stories can be preserved. One parent volunteer, a first generation Holocaust survivor, helped with the planning of the week's activities. Because of the heavy emotional impact of hearing survivors and death camp liberators speak, she suggested that a psychiatrist conduct the last library forum to help student gain a perspective about all that they had heard. This was a suggestion well taken.

In 1991, the central theme was the Native American. The book selected to serve as a basis for the study was

Highwater, Jamake. 1984. *Words in The Blood: Contemporary Indian Writers of North and South America.* New York: New American Library.

Library forums involved numerous Native Americans as can be seen in the faculty memos that are included in the Appendix. One of the highlights of the week was to team Native American senior citizens with high school seniors for one-on-one oral history interviews in the library. The students had prepared questions concerning what it was like to grow up as a Native American. After the interviews were edited, the class desktop published a booklet and gave copies to the Native Americans.

Ethnic Week 1992 dealt with Asian-American cultures with an emphasis on the Hmong. The literary source was

Moore, David L. 1989. *Dark Sky, Dark Land: Stories of the Hmong Boy Scouts of Troop 100.* Eden Prairie, Minnesota: Tessera Publishing Inc.

One of the major library forums featured Scoutmaster David Moore from Minneapolis, Minnesota, and Yee Chang and Chu Vue, two of the Boy Scouts highlighted in the book. They held student audiences spellbound as they told their stories of escape from their homeland to freedom in the United States. They also documented stories of Hmong life in Laos during the Vietnam War, their escape to Thailand, arrival in the United States as refugees and the adjustments to American society. Their tales reflect intense struggle, perseverance, love and ultimate victory to obtain freedom. Mary K. Chelton (Associate Editor, *Voice of Youth Advocates*) shared story cloths and other Hmong art work for exhibit. Another interesting aspect of the week brought twenty Japanese exchange college students to be interviewed in the library by high school seniors about life in Japan. At a time that the media headlines described Japan "bashing" our students got another point-of-view.

In the early 1960s, Dr. Marilyn Miller (President of the American Library Association, 1992-1993) taught a summer school course in school librarianship at the Library School, Emporia State University, Emporia, Kansas. In addition to being a very practical course, she instilled in me four ideas that have guided me for these thirtysome years. She said that school librarians must keep abreast of curriculum; we must adapt to the new technologies; we must insist that service to students and teachers come before everything else, even filing cards in the card catalog; and we must care about those young adults who attend our school, She said that if we followed those directives that program success could result and we might even change one young adult's life in a positive manner. I remember thinking to myself that I wanted to change thousands of lives, but she continued by saying that perhaps that is all one person could do in this life—to change another person's life positively. Somehow, I have never forgotten her words. In the summer after the first Ethnic Week concerning Apartheid was completed, a student who heard Prexy Nesbitt speak got a part-time job with the State Department of Education. Her task was to assist with clerical duties concerning a tri-state educational meeting being held in a Holiday Inn in St. Louis. She was in charge of making room reservations. She remembered that Mr. Nesbitt had said that Holiday Inn supported the South African government. The student told her supervisor that she could not morally make those reservations and she told him why. He responded and changed the location. Now I know that action did not hurt Holiday Inn, but she spoke out about her feelings and newfound awareness because of an experience that had its beginnings in the school's library. I couldn't help but wonder if the young lady who changed the motel reservations might be the one Marilyn Miller had in mind.

—Mike Printz

Chapter 2
Finding the Path

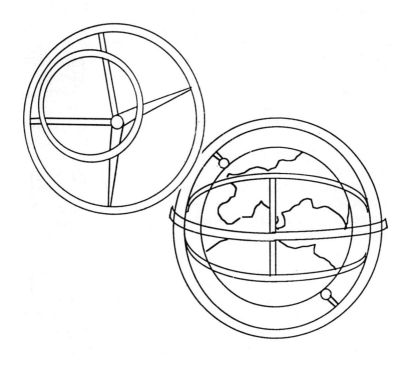

Mark Levy
Computer Graphics

Teaching Cultural Diversity

Teachers of the arts and literature are always willing and happy to share their love of the subject they are teaching with students in a variety of courses across the curriculum. We want students to know what we know: that art and literature help us to know ourselves and our fellow human beings. Since the first Ethnic Week library forums at Topeka West in 1988, students have used the study of particular works of literature to broaden their knowledge of the real world in which they live. They have discovered that they are part of something much larger than Topeka West High School, the greater Topeka urban community, and Kansas. They have learned that they share their hopes, dreams, and futures, with others whom they would never have known or cared about except through this literature. In this discovery of divergent others, students have learned that what they do can and does impact people they may never have known existed. They have learned that their voices matter to others worlds away. And our students have learned that they are an important part of a global community. In a recent article in *Educational Leadership*, James A. Banks states that "Education within a pluralistic society should affirm and help students understand their home and community cultures...[and] should help students acquire the knowledge, attitudes, and skills they will need to participate in civic action to make society more equitable and just." In realizing their importance and their connection to this world community, Topeka West High School students have come to appreciate and understand the power of the arts and its far-reaching impact. Happily, students have also discovered that different disciplines across the curricular spectrum do indeed enhance one another and that what is taught in each area is important to a complete understanding of a given subject. This came about because of the cooperation between Diane Goheen and Mike Printz, our librarians, and the teachers involved in the library forums.

This integrated approach served as the inspiration for our title, *Cultural Cobblestones: Teaching Cultural Diversity* because the purpose of this book is to provide pathways to cultural enrichment which can be used in any classroom. Our hopes are to provide activities to enhance student involvement and offer enlightenment to their individual learning processes. With each of the detailed integrated units of study presented in this book we offer varied levels of learning activities to reach students of all backgrounds. We also used one or more selected pieces of literature as a basis to tie our studies together. For us, this selected reading provided a common understanding of the respective cultures being studied. Within the library forums, the various works of literature students studied came alive as we joined together in the library to learn about a given culture from those who are part of that culture, those who are authors who have written about that culture, and those whose work students have read, or who are "experts" in the understanding of that culture. And because something may be gained from knowing those individuals who had the greatest impact upon our students, these people are briefly described at the start of each odd numbered chapter beginning with Chapter 3. As the teachers involved planned these forums and Ethnic Week activities, we developed enthusiasm as new opportunities for team-teaching and tying together our individual course objectives and required units of study became a reality. This new interest in the learning process was reflected in a higher level of student involvement and better quality student work.

Theresa Steinlage is primarily a writing and literature teacher. Her hope is to help students throughout the curriculum understand the impact of written and oral literature upon culture, politics, and as an art form. Her goals are for students to learn to think critically, develop a sense of voice, a commitment to the power of their own writing, and a sense of audience which extends beyond themselves and their own community. In short, she wants students to see themselves as authors who can teach others through what they have created in their own written art. The seriousness of this teaching was expressed by one student when he stated that "I never understood why it was the poets and teachers who were made to suffer first and longest whenever totalitarian governments gain control of a country" until his participation in writing poetry as a result of a study of Apartheid.

Some of the writing activities presented in this book may be familiar to many teachers who use a "whole language" approach in teaching. However, because they are specifically designed and intended to be used with particular works of literature and to gain an understanding of particular groups of people, they have taken on a life of their own and have become uniquely suited to these particular texts. Also, these activities were not used within the confines of one academic discipline, but were used in a variety of art, current events, mythology, creative writing, honors freshman English, English essentials ("remedial" language arts), and even math classes. They are thus designed for, and intended to be used in, virtually any classroom setting in which the understanding of literature and the art of writing become for students an understanding of themselves, others, and the world.

Lynda Miller is an art educator and wants her students to explore cultures and their specific art forms as a new tool in understanding the diversity that exists today. Her hope is that students come to an understanding of other cultures from as many points of view as possible. She feels that the students should experience the culture they are studying socially, politically, environmentally, geographically, emotionally, historically, as well as contemporary issues. Besides using fiction, nonfiction, folklore, children's books and periodicals to motivate or capture students interests, she uses visual exemplars of the fine arts to assist students in gaining further knowledge about a given culture. Before expressing their experience of this culture through art, students are required to see, touch, feel, and taste the culture personally. The students are asked to evaluate the art forms used within a given culture, explain the purpose of each art form and proceed into a hands on related art activity based upon the selected literature. The activity chosen to express their new understanding and knowledge is determined by the resources on hand as well as the art forms significant to each culture.

Robert Godfrey wrote an article titled "Civilization, Education, and the Visual Arts: A Personal Manifesto" for *Phi Delta Kappan* (April, 1992, pp. 596-600). In this article, Godfrey states

> Art plays an integral role in civilizing a society and its members. If introduced early and incorporated regularly into instruction, art teaches us about our capacity to communicate ideas and feelings in a variety of modes and medias: to analyze data through analogy and illustration; to accept compromise, ambiguity, and differences as positive human traits; and to construct ethical standards of judgment and action. Works of art tell us where we have been, indicate where we are, and leave evidence for future generations to examine for their own education, enlightenment, and delight.

Godfrey goes on to say, "The visible remains of our historical past serve as sources of information about our world. Through the visual arts we can directly comment on the human condition and begin to comprehend the complexities of our species and of our multicultural society." The overall intent for this project is to provide each student with an opportunity to become a citizen of the world. It is to encourage visually talented young adults to seek out and touch this citizenship with a responsibility to communicate needed changes and share personal concerns with others through their art. And this knowledge began to develop through the reading of particular texts for each culture celebrated during Ethnic Week. If a picture is worth a thousand words, art should develop from at least the reading of as many as a thousand words as well.

Our team philosophy was to put ourselves as educators into the learning process along with our students. With teachers teaching teachers as well as students, all teachers involved served as role models as they participated with students in activities. In all four units of study presented in this book, students were asked to process their learning by reading the selected literature, creating a written reaction, and processing their learning into an art form that depicts an understanding of the culture they were studying. The format of the book reflects our team approach to teaching and our belief in the learning of our students. Beginning with Chapter 3, "Traveling a Twisted Path," odd-numbered chapters present language art and art activities as they were taught in our study of various cultures during Ethnic Week library forums throughout a four-year period. Beginning with Chapter 4, "Marking the Path into a Troubled Land," even-numbered chapters present student work that is the culmination of the learning that took place as a result of involvement in activities presented in the odd-numbered chapters. All student work is marked so that it is easy to see which activity is represented in a given work of art or writing.

And as you read and view what these students have accomplished, keep in mind that they represent a broad spectrum of abilities and talents. We deliberately selected materials which reflect the range of students represented in our classes. This range not only reflects ability levels but also our own multicultural student population that includes African-Americans, Mexican-Americans, the grandchildren of Holocaust survivors, Native Americans, Chinese, Koreans, Eastern Indians, South Americans, Malaysians, and Irish, Russian, French, Catholic, Jewish and Protestant European-Americans. All coming together in a beautiful kaleidoscope of students within a "typical" middle American high school.

Chapter 3

Traveling a Twisted Path
South African Apartheid

Lynda Miller

Mark Mathabane

Heroes help us to see the character or greatness of spirit or athletic excellence to which we all may aspire. Today there may seem to be a shortage of such individuals. And yet there are heroes. We just need to know how to recognize them. Mark Mathabane is someone whom upon first meeting would not appear heroic. He is a rather small, scholarly, mild young man who speaks of Wordsworth and honesty and staying true to yourself. He speaks of our connection to one another and the importance of understanding and compassion for those who are different than ourselves.

We had the extreme good fortune of meeting and listening to Mr. Mathabane in the summer of 1990 at an American Libraries Association conference in Chicago. We had read Mr. Mathabane's autobiography. He had become a hero for us because of his portrayal of his personal triumph over the injustice and evil of Apartheid. Mr. Mathabane's life is a lesson in the power of forgiveness and the strength of the human spirit and intellect.

Language Arts Activities for a Study of South Africa

Literature Base: *Somehow Tenderness Survives: Stories of Southern Africa*. Selected by Hazel Rochman

Somehow Tenderness Survives: Stories of Southern Africa, is a collection of autobiographical accounts and short stories which eloquently portray life under an absolutely unjust system of government. The selections are all understated in their portrayal of brutality. And in that understatement they serve as a powerful voice for the disenfranchised everywhere. It is a reader friendly text which could be used at every level from the eighth through twelfth grades and beyond. This book was used in a freshman English class and creative writing classes.

Because Hazel Rochman's selections convey so well the character of Apartheid through the human portrayal of the inhabitants of these narratives, the following objectives may be learned from a study of this book.

1. What bigotry is and what it means.
2. An empathy for South Africans.
3. A recognition of what we have in common with all South Africans.
4. The creation of the myth of superiority.
5. The power of literature to carry messages and convey circumstances.

These things are learned through an understanding of these stories, and because these stories are so engaging, understanding them also leads to an understanding of the short story and the following literary elements.

1. Characterization
2. Plot
3. Setting
4. Imagery
5. Suspense

These elements become important when taught in the context of a study of a real situation as students are also learning about the subject in art, social studies, and home economics classes. Thus the elements of plot (exposition, conflict, climax, and resolution) are seen as a reflection of the reality of our own and others' lives when set against the backdrop of the drama portrayed in the real conflict of Apartheid in South Africa. In their struggle to understand Apartheid, students came to understand bigotry in America at a deeper level as they asked the question "How could they?" only to discover "How could we?"

Procedures and Activities

We began our study of *Somehow Tenderness Survives* by discovering South Africa. We tapped the social studies department for information and with the help of Jeff Handley, who teaches current events and who was also involved in the library forum on South Africa, came to a better understanding of the South Africa which was being portrayed in the news. Also the library supplied all classes involved in Ethnic Week activities with a packet of current newspaper and magazine articles, pamphlets, and fact sheets about South Africa. Part of one class period was spent discussing South Africa. The rest of the time was spent on *Somehow Tenderness Survives* (one week); students came to their own conclusions and under-

standing by working through a series of writing assignments which
culminated in the publication of their own anthology of poems and
observations of not only South Africa, but the human condition. Through
this process, they developed into authors with a sense of purpose, audience, and voice.

After the initial lecture, students were formed into small groups (five
students was the maximum). Each student was required to read one
newspaper article (provided by the library) and simply tell others within
their group what they learned about South Africa from that article. A
"secretary" was appointed by each group to write down approximately
three facts learned by the group from each member's summary. At the
conclusion of the class period, the group secretaries were to share what
their group had learned about South Africa with the entire class. This
sharing was tape recorded. The next day, the tape was played back to the
students. Then the students began a reading journal for *Somehow Tenderness Survives* by writing down everything they knew about South Africa
in a fifteen minute span of time. Following this, students began reading.

The Reading Journal

Reading journals require students to write about something they are
reading. The reason for assigning a reading journal is to provide students
with an independent, private, secure place to think and write critically and
creatively about a given text. *Somehow Tenderness Survives* lends itself
easily to a journal where students discover for themselves the literary and
cultural elements present. Students were asked to read the book in its
entirety beginning with the first story and ending with the last. Students
wrote assigned journal entries to be completed within their week long
study of this book. Students wrote these in ink on loose-leaf notebook
paper using both sides of the page but not having more than one selection
from the book represented on any one side of a sheet of paper. Students
were also asked to address particular statements or questions intended as
prompts to focus their writing. They were asked to copy these statements
and questions from the chalkboard and place this sheet of paper at the
front of their journals. They were also told that the journals were to be
legible but that they were not going to be graded on written conventions
or the length of their entries. Most of their entries were over a page in
length. The following are the prompts used by students to complete their
journals. The literary elements addressed by each entry are in parentheses.

"Crackling Day" by Peter Abrahams
(setting, characterization).

After you have read this story, close your eyes for a moment and pretend you are the character Uncle Sam. Now write a letter to your nephew explaining the beating. In your letter, explain how you feel. Tell what your dreams are for his future. Tell how WHERE you are (your setting) has affected how you and your nephew must live. Be certain to use details from the selection to help with your case.

"Old Chief Mshlanga" by Doris Lessing
(plot, characterization, suspense).

Write why you think the narrator in this story suddenly shifts from the third person to the first person point of view in the middle of the narrative. What does this shift in point of view tell you about the character of the narrator and the changes which have taken place in her? Do you sympathize with her? Why or why not?

"A Day in the Country" by Dan Jacobson
(characterization, plot).

Once again close your eyes for a few minutes. This time imagine you are the Jewish father who has just returned home after witnessing the cruel game depicted in this story. It is night and you are saying your evening prayers. Write a prayer you think this character might pray the night he witnessed this game.

"Country Lovers" by Nadine Gordimer
(setting).

Suppose the baby in this story had survived into childhood. If you were a lawyer for the baby, how would you argue for her rights?

"When the Train Comes" by Zoe Witcomb
(characterization, setting, plot, suspense).

Continue this story by writing the next scene. What do you think is going to happen to the narrator once she reaches school?

"The Toilet" by Gcina Mhlope
(setting, characterization, suspense).

Describe your favorite place to be alone and escape your troubles. How important is reading and writing to you? Do you have a room of your own? What do you have in common with this narrator?

"The Road to Alexandra" by Mark Mathabane
(setting, characterization, imagery).

Write for five minutes about your most vivid memory from the year you were five years old. What is the one greatest difference between your life at the age of five and Mark Mathabane's recollection of the year he was five?

"A Chip of Glass Ruby" by Nadine Gordimer
(characterization, setting).

If you were one of Mrs. Bamjee's children would you consider your mother a hero or a villain? Why or why not?

"A Farm at Raraba" by Ernst Havermann
(setting, imagery).

Write a brief scene in which you depict the black soldier's dream coming true. Why is it only a dream?

"It's Quiet Now" by Gcina Mhlope
(plot, characterization, setting).

If you've been paying attention, you've probably noticed that there is a progression within this book; that taken as a whole, it becomes a story formed from stories. Why do you suppose that Hazel Rochman chose to conclude this book with this particular selection?

Following the completion of a week of reading and journal writing, students were again formed into groups. All students were asked to read the journal entry they felt was the most insightful or their favorite aloud to the other members. The group then selected the reading they thought would be of help to others in the class and each of these was read aloud to the entire class at the end of the period. The journals were then turned in for evaluation. They were evaluated according to three criteria: *Thoroughness.* Did they complete the assignment for all ten selections from the book? *Creativity.* Did their journal display original thought? Or was it merely a retelling of the text? *Understanding.* Did each of their journal entries show an insight into the story regarding one or more of the following elements: characterization, plot, setting, imagery, or suspense? It is important to note that these criteria for evaluation were given to the students prior to their ever beginning their journals.

The Biopoem

Using their reading journals as a starting point, students were required to write a "Biopoem" based upon one of the characters from any of the ten selections. Prior to giving students this assignment, they were told that their biopoems would be evaluated according to how they had stated the feelings, dreams, and soul of the character they chose to write about. A biopoem that only states facts has not succeeded. But a biopoem that causes us to feel what another may feel or see what another may see is successful. What follows is a copy of the assignment given to students (adapted from "The Course Journal" by Pat Juell in the book *Roots in the Sawdust: Writing to Learn Across the Disciplines,* edited by Anne Ruggles Gere, National Council of the Teachers of English, 1985):

A biopoem requires you think about the "essence" of a specific thing. In each stage of its development, ideas are being selected, formulated, and clarified. The finished poem is a summative written portrait. In deciding what should be included in this portrait, you are allowed to make decisions about what is important about a character from literature through inquiry in which the questions are as important as the answers.

A biopoem may follow this pattern, but remember this is only a starting point. Work with this pattern and the information it provides you to create your own *unique* poem representing the character who most intrigued you within this book.

Line 1. First Name
Line 2. Four traits that describe this character
Line 3. Relative of (brother, sister, daughter, etc.)
Line 4. Lover of (list three things)
Line 5. Who feels (list three things)
Line 6. Who fears (list three things)
Line 7. Who needs (list three things)
Line 8. Who gives (list three things)
Line 9. Who would like to see (list three things)
Line 10. Resident of (where does he/she reside. Be creative!)
Line 11. Last Name (or a summative statement of the significance of your subject)

The biopoems written by students were put together into a booklet that was displayed in the library and given to each of the students who had a biopoem published in it. These biopoems are noteworthy examples of how sensitive, insightful, and creative high school students can be.

Literature Base: *Kaffir Boy*
by Mark Mathabane

Procedures and Activities

One of the most moving narratives in *Somehow Tenderness Survives* is Mark Mathabane's description of the night his father was arrested in "The Road to Alexandra." The freshman English students followed their study of Hazel Rochman's anthology with the book *Kaffir Boy* by Mark Mathabane. This book is one of the best autobiographical accounts available to literature teachers. Its literary merit alone would make it worth acquiring for use in any language arts classroom. No one has ever told their story any more eloquently than Mr. Mathabane tells his. This autobiography that is appropriate for grades nine through twelve, is must reading for any student or teacher who wants to understand the challenge Apartheid and other systems of exploitation and degradation pose for the human spirit. This was reason enough to have students read this book. Yet, because of the graphic portrayal of violence, a homosexual brothel, and the degradation depicted in *Kaffir Boy*, there is a need to inform parents about the text and obtain their permission prior to assigning it to students to read. Whenever a text may prove painful to students or their parents, open, honest communication is imperative to the successful teaching of the text.

However, *Kaffir Boy* is too well written and rich in content not to use as a vehicle for teaching literary elements and the power of the truth the art of writing may convey. Students began the study of *Kaffir Boy* by thinking about what they would write about their own lives. This is an autobiographical account, and in writing an autobiography the author cannot possibly write every event which he/she has experienced. Rather, the author of an autobiography picks and chooses the events from his/her life that will reveal the most to the reader about that life. Students drew maps of what their lives have been. They considered these questions as they drew the maps of their personal journeys through life: "Were there hills and valleys? Mountains? Was your life ever a desert? In the middle of the desert was there ever an oasis?" Students completed this activity using markers and typing paper. It is a fun activity. And as they complete it, students are forced to consider their own lives. We created a display on the bulletin board of those maps from students who didn't mind sharing them. Students thought about what they chose to put on their maps and why they chose those things. We then began a journal centered on the book *Kaffir Boy* by continuing to focus upon ourselves. Before students were given this book they wrote for five minutes (fifteen minutes total) about: "My Parents, My Home, and My Education." Student responses were not evaluated on punctuation, spelling, or other written conventions but rather on the students' commitment to writing for five full minutes about the topics provided.

The Reading Journal

Autobiographical Comparison/Contrast Essay

For their next journal assignment, students folded papers in half vertically to create two columns in which they wrote. On the left-hand side they wrote about specific problems or questions they encountered as they read the book. These problems or encounters did not necessarily have to be in understanding the text, but rather may have been what students were discovering about life under Apartheid through reading the text. Students wrote about their life as it paralleled Mr. Mathabane's on the right hand side of the page in a different color of ink. They were to complete a minimum of ten journal entries. (However, the power of this book and the story it tells are so compelling that seldom did a student turn in less than a fifteen-page journal. Their engagement with this text was immediate and profound.) After they had completed their reading of this text and writing their journals, students completed a comparison/contrast essay in which they compared their life to the life of Mark Mathabane. (See Josh Stuart's essay in Chapter 4.)

This book had such an emotional pull for students that it was not uncommon for many of them to go on independently to read the sequel, *Kaffir Boy in America*. Mark Mathabane's life and his family members "and what happened to them next?" came to matter to these students because the people who populate this autobiography are so vividly portrayed that they come to life for the students who read about them.

Creative Writing

It was not a difficult decision to include creative writing classes in Ethnic Week activities for South Africa. This was an opportunity for student poets to understand the power of poetry. We began with a study of "Found Poetry."

Because they don't have to think of the words but "find" them in someone else's text, found poetry is a wonderful way to introduce poetry to students. As they select precise words from the text of another author to form their own poem, it also helps students to understand that words are the medium for the poet as an artist. The original text takes on new meaning once words are "found" and reworked by the student poet/artist.

Students began by writing five facts they knew about South Africa. These facts did not need to be good or bad but simply statements of what their personal knowledge was of South Africa. In doing this, students began thinking about what they knew and their curiosity was piqued as they also discovered what they didn't know about South Africa. They then formed small groups (no smaller than three or larger than four) and each group formed a new list based upon a consensus of what the group thought was true about South Africa. Each group selected a member to write their community list on the chalkboard. The order of this collective list was then reworked through the consensus of the entire class until everyone was satisfied it formed a poem.

The following class period, students were supplied with pamphlets, magazine, and newspaper articles in the form of a Library Information

Packet as material for their own found poetry. Each student was given something to read about South Africa. After they had been allowed to read their material, students once again returned to their groups to work. This time they were to share their articles with their group members. The group selected the most interesting article to share with the entire class. They did this to enrich their knowledge of, and empathy for, South Africa, and it was an amazingly effective way of doing so. It contributed to the atmosphere of sharing to form a large circle so that students were all facing one another. What emerged in this sharing of the "most interesting" articles, was the realization that there is a tremendous power in simply stating facts.

The rest of the week was spent by the students working on their own found poetry. They were allowed (even encouraged) to work in groups as they discovered which articles they wanted to use, as they selected the words that would become their poems. and as they did the final word processing in preparation for displaying their poetry.

Publication occurred when students displayed their typewritten texts on the bulletin board in the library during Ethnic Week. My students decided to mat their poems on black-and-white construction paper cut on a diagonal and separated by a red strip of construction paper. The matting itself made a powerful statement and showed students had indeed learned to see their poetry as an art. (See Chapter 4 for student exemplars.)

Art Activities for a Study of South Africa

Literature Base: *Somehow Tenderness Survives: Stories of Southern Africa.* Selected by Hazel Rochman.

To start this South African Apartheid study, it was explained to the art students that they were going to have to develop a knowledge base. The student assignment was to read *Somehow Tenderness Survives: Stories of Southern Africa* and then look over the packet of current information and historical information developed by our two librarians and parent volunteers. Following this reading, the students were asked to *restate* their new knowledge on South Africa and the Apartheid movement into a written form. After they completed their writing, the students were asked to create a visual *reaction* of what they had learned during this investigative cultural unit.

As an art teacher, it is important to clarify the terms *restate* and *react*. When students *restate* their information they are to write a summary, a listing of events, or map out specific events that can be developed into a visual expression. The restatements may answer such questions as: Where is this taking place? Why is this happening? Who is it happening to? What can be done to correct this activity? What emotions are involved in this injustice? Who is most affected by this injustice? The student's restatement is the sharing of knowledge gained, while their *reaction* serves to demonstrate how it makes them feel. Reactions ask for personal feelings, judgments and require individual self expression to their chosen subject matter. The student's reaction is an activity that develops not only new knowledge but also demonstrates a personal involvement with the subject being addressed in their art work.

Procedures and Activities

The art students were each handed a copy of *Somehow Tenderness Survives* and read the quote by Nelson Mandela, and the poem by Dennis Brutus, "Somehow We Survive." We also discussed our involvement with the Ethnic Week project which would be taking place at our school. The students were asked to read one of the ten short stories in the book. They could choose any story as long as all of the short stories were chosen by someone in the class. We read over the contents of the book and no more than four students signed up to read any one story. Reading in the art classroom prior to creating a visual image is not a typical procedure. The students at first felt this part of the assignment too academic (not an activity that they relished) and that is why each student was required to read only one story. However, Hazel Rochman's book is so well written, that the student attitudes changed and their desire to learn more information on South Africa became more positive and focused. After their initial involvement with this book, most of the students read the entire book and many shared it with friends and family as well.

Upon completion of the reading assignment, the students restated their assigned story in several ways. First, the students filled out a worksheet outlining the story, and were asked to answer the following questions.

Student Restatement Sheet

1. Who were the main characters in your story?
2. What was the main event in the story?
3. What was the purpose of the story?
4. What was the setting, season, or time of day in your story?
5. Draw any visual pictures or images that you could see while reading this story.

After each student had completed the worksheet, all students who had read the same short story were asked to discuss their answers with each other. A booktalk about each story followed and that is when the students started to read the other stories. A second worksheet was then provided to further student interest following this discussion. This second worksheet was designed to encourage the development of student emotional involvement or to create a student reaction. The following questions were asked on the second worksheet.

Student Reaction Worksheet

1. What was your reaction to the story?
2. What part of your story could be created into a visual picture or illustration?
3. What colors or lines could be used to help depict the emotional impact of this story?
4. What did the setting, environment, or terrain look like?
5. What was the author's intent in writing this story?
6. Start to compile a running list of subject matter that you need to research as you develop an illustration of this story.

The last activity on this worksheet was to reread or look through the story again and make a list of at least twenty-five descriptive phrases that created for them a visual picture as they read *Somehow Tenderness Survives*.

The student assignments were to complete one written project and two visual projects during this unit of study of Apartheid. The written project was in an "artistic" form of found poetry. Using the twenty-five phrases selected from the second worksheet, the students were asked to write a poem using the visual images found within their selected story. The art students were told that they could alter, change, or repeat their found phrases to make their poems more expressive and personal. This form of writing truly assists the student in developing a visual form as the poetry provides the student with too much imagery and the students have to eliminate ideas rather than find more information to draw. Most of the time, the student's visual compositions are richer and more expressive after a writing assignment. This assignment took about two hours, however, many students wrote and rewrote their poems several times before they felt that they had said what really needed to be said. Below is a teaching exemplar of the twenty-five phrases and how the students created their poems.

List of phrases from "The Road to Alexandra" by Mark Mathabane

1. back-back raids
2. gripped by rumors
3. street by street, yard by yard
4. ghetto of gangsters and prostitutes
5. undesirables
6. hanging over like a dark cloud
7. always scared
8. dogs barked
9. sirens screamed
10. children screamed
11. tightening in the pit of my stomach
12. open up
13. darkness was ominous
14. flashlights flared
15. glass shattered
16. one kicked me savagely
17. stars in my eyes
18. begging for forgiveness
19. bloodied hands
20. his self-esteem drained
21. manhood sapped
22. emotional nakedness
23. tears surge to my eyes
24. papa
25. handcuffed men and women

The following is an example of a poem that I wrote and modeled for my students from phrases found in "The Road to Alexandra" by Mark Mathabane.

Papa

Small children,
    scared,
    living in a ghetto, a dark cloud
    gripped by rumors of back to back raids.

As the darkness fell, the dogs started to bark,
    sirens screamed.

The darkness becomes more ominous
    as voices yell, "Open up!".
Flashlights flared from undesirables,
    "Open up!".

PAPA!

Glass shattered.

PAPA!

One kicked me savagely and stars took over.

As I knelt begging for forgiveness
    their flashlights flared on my bloodied hands.

They grabbed my PAPA.

Handcuffed his self esteem,
    sapped him of his manhood.

They left ... he left....
    yard by yard....
    street by street ... into emotional nakedness.

The children screamed.

Tears surge to my eyes.

PAPA?

Upon the completion of reading and reacting to the story and after experiencing the opportunity to restate their selected story in a written form, the students had gained a better understanding of the author's intent and were ready to move to a higher level of sharing this knowledge.

To move from the verbal, cognitive mode of thinking and shift to a visual, affective format of expression, the students were asked to "take a line for a walk." This art activity was adapted from "Walking the Line," by Nicholas Roukes from *Design Synectics: Stimulating Creativity in Design* (p. 79). This activity simply asks the student to restate the story line in a visual format. The students were asked to draw the images that came to mind as they rethought the story with a single line. Using a sheet of large unlined drawing paper and a pencil, the students drew one continuous line using words, images or symbols to tell the story and their reactions to the events that took place in the story. This classroom activity can be completed in two different fashions. First, it can be done individually and the completed work serves as an illustration for each student's individual poem or story. Or secondly, the line walk can be done individually and then connected with the lines created by all of the other students to illustrate the entire book as a mural. The latter project works best when the students include their poems into the line as it makes the mural more interesting and provides the observer with the necessary tools for a greater understanding of each of the ten stories. The classtime spent on this project was two hours.

This mural activity works well with markers, pastels, and large rolled paper. The students need to feel that they cannot make a mistake and that all expressions are correct. When asking for student reactions, or visually expressive value judgments, it is essential to treat these expressions with care. Everyone has a right to express themselves without criticism. A practice page may be helpful and the students create better when they do not talk. Quiet music in the background is helpful, something with a South African motif may serve as a motivating device. To create their final project, the students need to draw their lines on the paper first, and then go back and add color, texture, excerpts or all of their poem. Encourage the students to add repetition in line forms, and to vary the line width for interest. An example of "taking a line for a walk" follows.

Hilary Porterfield, Line Drawing

With the mural project, the students need to feel ownership to their part of the mural as well as to the overall finished piece. This ownership takes place by allowing the students to enhance any part of the mural after the original lines and writings have been added. The final stage of this project would be an evaluation and sharing process. All students gain additional points of view on the given subject matter through the mural activity. The final critique of the mural provides two important learning activities: one, the positive sharing of one another's involvement with this project, and two, an opportunity for the students to write their reactions to the project. This last activity was an overall evaluation of the project and this student input serves the staff well in planning and implementing future projects.

The second art assignment for the students to complete was a visual project (realistic or abstract) depicting the emotional aspect of their selected story. To help the students develop this illustration, we needed to do further research in the library. The students were encouraged to look for more information on South Africa, its people, its problems, especially noting the subject matter that they had outlined as essential for their story from their previously completed worksheets. A record of all new information gathered during their research was kept in a sketchbook format and the final composition was created from this sketchbook.

The librarians were available, willing and instrumental here in encouraging students to research. With their resources and the upcoming forums, which included speakers who were knowledgeable about Apartheid in South Africa, the students were determined to make personal statements in their work. These statements were to demonstrate an understanding of not only the stories read, but also the injustices that the students had recently learned about.

Because the students were enrolled in different art courses, their final projects were completed in different media. The drawing students worked in pastels, and the printmaking students worked in linoleum and aquatints.

The students had investigated rituals, ceremonies, symbols, traditional dress, art forms, housing, terrains, environments, features of the South Africans, animals, religions, foods and music. We had the students taste, touch and feel what it would be like to be South African in every manageable method possible from a midwestern American location. The finished art work was placed on display in our library to be viewed by the student body during the Ethnic Week activities. Because of the completed art work, the art students that attended the library forums were more receptive to the speakers and to the topics discussed. As their art teacher, I felt pride in the excellent questions they asked and their individual sensitivity to the problems of the Apartheid movement in South Africa.

The staff and students involved in this Ethnic Week project felt that it was a great success. What surprised us the most were the attitudes conveyed by our guest speakers. They were amazed at the genuine interest and concern our students displayed at the forums, and as a result helped to implement as additional learning experience for all of us during the next semester of school.

The second forum presentation was to serve as an update on the Apartheid movement and to provide our students with the opportunity to work with internationally known artist/muralist from Mozambique, Malangatana Valente Ngwenya. The art activity developed for students during this forum was intended to include approximately one-hundred-and-twenty-five art students and fifty creative writing students. We developed a mural depicting the stories once again from *Somehow Tenderness Survives*. Students were divided up into ten groups and each group worked together while reading their specific stories. The first part of their assignment was to restate their story in a physical form. The students were asked to create a dramatic masterpiece by placing themselves into a posed picture or a composition that could convey the following: the objects and physical characters in the story, the setting for the story, and the emotional impact of the story. The student groups developed costuming and a set for each masterpiece (ten in all). We photographed each masterpiece developed and then proceeded to create a mural using the photographs as guides to proportion and placement of the characters. When the mural was designed it depicted all ten short stories from *Somehow Tenderness Survives*.

The mural was created on large rolled butcher paper attached to the library basement walls (approximately 8 feet by 40 feet). The student compositions were transferred to the mural in line form and were life-size in scale. The students could actually see themselves in the mural wearing the traditional dress of those they were learning about. At this point we had an outline of the mural completed, and the student enthusiasm and individual ownership to this project became stronger. The next activity involved art and creative writing students. We asked the students to add additional decorative lines to the mural in order to create texture and all students placed their creative writing onto the mural. All line work and creative writing was done in black magic marker. The selection of brown butcher paper and black markers helped create an African feeling as it was intended to represent the bark cloth used by early African artists.

Before completing our final activity, to add color and emotion to the mural, the students were introduced to our guest artist/muralist, Malangatana Ngwenga. He would best be described as a sensitive, gentle, grandfatherly man with large expressive eyes, which projected the emotions of those around him as fast as they grasped the same information.

During his visit to the Untied States, he had spoken to many businesses, organizations, and interested groups about Apartheid and all of these presentations had been factual in nature. Malangatana was scheduled to be at only one high school throughout all of his travels; and we wanted his experience at Topeka West High School to be a positive one for him, as well as an educational opportunity for our students. During his stay with us, Malangatana was first made aware of our mural project and that his role with this project was simply to work with the students.

We explained to Malangatana that his student audience was well informed about Apartheid in South Africa. However, the students needed insight to a more sensitive, humanistic point of view of South Africa and Mozambique. He was told that while they needed to learn how the people of Mozambique were affected by Apartheid, the students also needed to hear first-hand about the spirit of his people, their traditions, customs and beliefs. He seemed excited about providing a presentation that would allow his personal feelings to be expressed. Malangatana was asked to share stories with students that his grandmother had told him when he was a little boy. He spoke to us of the beauty of his land and of the unique qualities of his people. Malangatana told us of his personal hopes and dreams for his country. He did not dwell on the human suffering or tragedies, but on the celebrations and seldom heard priviledged bits of information about the people of Mozambique. The artist in Malangatana truly related well with the students as they acted out some of his stories and sang songs with him.

All students involved were excused from their afternoon classes and we worked together for approximately three hours completing this mural. As all of the students, teachers, librarians and Malangatana put on work aprons and used pastels to add emotion and color to the mural, everyone had a new insight to share and having our guest artist only enhanced that experience. It was amazing how quickly the students felt that he had ownership into the mural that was equal to their own. This was an unforgettable educational experience for everyone involved. Our guest artist was exceptionally talented, warm, honest, caring and full of information to share with us all. To simply say, "thank you" to Malangatana would never be enough for the inspiration he provided to all of us on that day.

Our mural created during this project was later taken apart and made into twelve two-by-four-foot panels. One panel was given to Prexy Nesbitt. One panel was given to Hazel Rochman, author of *Somehow Tenderness Survives*. Another panel was given to Mark Mathabane, author of "Road to Alexandra," one of the selections in *Somehow Tenderness Survives* and taken from his book, *Kaffir Boy*. One panel was sent to Malangatana Ngwenya, African artist from Mozambique. Three of the panels were copied and used as our school district's Christmas card. (See Chapter 3 title page.)

This overall project has served us well as it touched others who have touched us and it has created a larger audience of awareness for our concerns about Apartheid.

Chapter 4

Marking the Path Into a Troubled Land: South African Apartheid

Christi Furnas, Pen and Ink

Jason Gilbert, Linoleum Print

Alexandra and Topeka
by Josh Shuart
(*Kaffir Boy.* Comparison/Contrast Essay)

Two beings in time, separated by fate. They are both human beings with unique qualities and gifts, each with their own interests and desires; both created equal. One, by a mere quirk of fate, is brought to the city of Topeka, Kansas, in a free country called America. Little does he know that he is one of the lucky few in the world today who will never be segregated or picked on by his government. He can roam freely as he wishes, go anywhere without having to possess a pass, and can board any bus and use any public phone or restroom that he wishes. As he gets older, he takes all these rights and privileges for granted, for that is all he knows. He has never heard of the word "Apartheid." He gets anything from his parents that he wishes: bicycles, computers, stereos, color TVs, VCRs, basketball goals, and a car to name a few. Expensive clothes and shoes are considered boring. He complains if he does not get everything he wants. His parents are both well educated and successful. Life to him is nothing but a bed of roses.

The other being in time who loses this genetic coin toss is not nearly as fortunate. He is brought to a vicious, dirty, diseased, poverty stricken, and decrepit ghetto in the town of Alexandra, South Africa. Little does he know that he is one of the unfortunate few in the world who lives as a fourth class being. As he gets older, he comes to the shocking and horrifying realization that he will not be able to get a decent education; use the same trains, buses, public restrooms, drinking fountains, and phones as white people; or walk anywhere without having a pass permitting him to be there. He must go to sleep at night on a wet, soggy, rotten piece of cardboard with newspapers as blankets. During the day he must beg, loot, and take from the dump in order to get enough food to eat. But usually he fails miserably. To keep from starving, he must either become a ruthless gang member, called a tsotsi, and kill and steal, or he can prostitute himself to homosexuals and receive food and money in return for committing unnatural acts.

The similarities between these two beings are many. They are both gifted in their own special ways. Love and affection is both offered and needed by each. Both have dreams and goals. Both have feelings. Both are products of their environment, and they are BOTH human beings.

It is a shame that a simple twist of fate would place one in a world of wealth, equality, and love and the other in a living hell of hunger, segregation, poverty, and death. Every single white in America has a twin in South Africa, like negatives to a roll of film. The time has come when we begin showing that we care.

Natalie Martin, Pastels

Little Black
by Kara Van Cleaf
(Biopoem. *Somehow Tenderness Survives,* "Crackling Day")

Little
Black
scared, young, helpless
Loves
his family, time with loved ones
Feels
anger, rage, pity
Needs
love, companions,
Fears
prejudice, hatred
Gives
all he can
Wants to see

> equality,
> love,
> a normal life
> South African
> Boy

Lynda Miller

Mother of a South African Family
by Wendy Whiteside
(Biopoem. *Somehow Tenderness Survives,* "Crackling Day")

Love is given out in large quantities to HER FAMILY
She feels useless in helping HER FAMILY
She NEEDS HER FAMILY
Fearing white people, punishment, and losing HER FAMILY
She gives a feeling of meekness, but it's a front,
                    FOR HER FAMILY
On the inside she's strong and knows Apartheid is WRONG ...
BUT WON'T TAKE A STAND, for her family

One woman facing an epidemic of unfairness WITH HER FAMILY!!!

Larry Morford, Acrylic Painting

Father
By Michael Book
(Biopoem. *Somehow Tenderness Survives,* **"A Day in the Country")**

I am a father,
I am a farmer and Jew,
But I am also a South African,
And I am white, but not free.
How can I show my children the truth?
They know who I am.
They know my love for God,
For peace,
For people.
Can I teach them to feel my compassion,
My anger,
My loss?
Will they need what I do?
Family,
Peace of mind,
Freedom?
Do they know how I fear our countrymen's ignorance,
Their repression,
Their stubborness? All that I can hope to give them is my knowledge,
My example,
My hope.

My only wish is to see in them the evils undone,
To see new life in them,
To see a desire for unity in them.
I am a father.
A resident of oppression,
Of hatred,
Of pain.
I can only hope to be their faithful teacher,
An example of man's true soul.
I am a father.

Autobiographical Map
by Kate Gilliland
(Journal. *Kaffir Boy*)

This Is Apartheid
by Jennifer Stephens
(Free Verse. Library Information Packet.)

South Africa
a black and white world
where pain and sadness
embitter the bleak
grey lives

of innocents branded,
and spit on.
A world where hopes and dreams are crushed
as villages

are raided,
and destroyed,
and with them their haven
from the blistering storm
of ugly Apartheid.
Sun City,
a disgusting symbol of bigotry
and prejudice,
washing itself clean in a river of tears
shed by children
whose families are missing,
imprisoned,
murdered.
This is Apartheid.

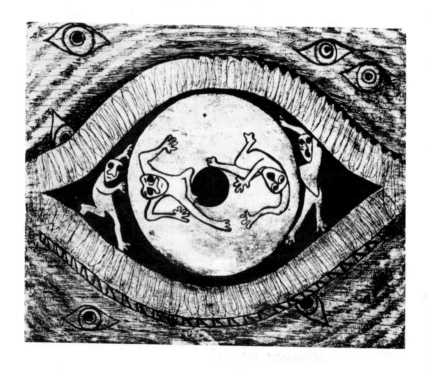

Heather Nolte, "River Of Tears," Aquatint

A White Man's Game
By Katharine Humphrey
(Biopoem, *Somehow Tenderness Survives*, "Country Lovers")

I'm a little black girl
I'm scared, confused, angry, and full of doubts.
Of all the things I hate, I hate white men the most
Of all the things I love, I'm told to say I love white men the
most
I fear the white men because of the games they sometimes like to
play with us
sometimes they're cruel
Yes, sometimes they're cruel
I scream,
They laugh,
I cry
They laugh
Of all the things I hate, I hate white men the most
Of all the things I love, I love white men the most
Scared, confused, angry, and full of doubts
I'm a little black girl in South Africa.

Shawn Martin, Aquatint

Religious Revolt
By Chris Bloxsom
(Found Poem. Library Information Packet.)

A dramatic
confrontation between
church and state
occurred when 17
anti apartheid
organizations
marched on parliament
police arrested them
including
Archbishop TuTu.
They water cannoned
others.
After a brief detention
an angry Tutu said
"We are going to embark on a
course of
civil disobedience."
In response
our government
introduced legislation
to limit foreign aid.
The government of
South Africa
clearly set itself on a
collision course
with the Church of
Christ.
The state President
should pay heed to the
words of
Jesus:
The Gates of
Hell
will never hold out against
The Church.

Struggle
by Chanee Livingston
(Found Poem. Library Information Packet.)

Struggle for
equality.

Racial unrest.

They're trying
to kill an idea ...

black
consciousness.

Emily Eakes, Pen and Ink

Journal Entries
by Greg Thayer
(*Kaffir Boy*)

Chapter 27
First Response

What are hostels? I know it is the word "hotel" comes from, but is that the appropriate meaning for this instance?

Why did the fleeing man think he would get help from the people in the nearby shacks? Surely he knew that they wouldn't want to intervene for fear of their own lives.

Mark's reaction to the murder answers his own questions about the constant killings in the black ghettos. He withdraws from life, not caring whether he lives or dies. And if one doesn't care about their own life, why would they be expected to care for the lives of others? This condition could easily lead to the life of a tsotsi.

Second Response

The first difference in this chapter is the relative importance of birthdays. They haven't the money to celebrate it, as is done elsewhere.

Mark states that he feels that life in Alexandra is just getting worse, while I feel that life in general is getting better.

Such raw violence is often seen on TV, but I have never (and hopefully won't) seen anything at all similar to the murder Mark witnesses.

Chapter 28
First Response

It's almost surprising that Mark hadn't been feeling this way before, considering the awful conditions he lived under. But I suppose that since he had nothing in his experience to compare it to, he couldn't realize how bad off he really was. His mother's constant encouragement gave him the hope to continue, but the murder extinguished his hope.

My admiration for Mrs. Mathabane went up another notch when I read how she handled Mark's suicide attempt. I think to a large extent Mark's accomplishments should be duly credited to her efforts to bring him up well despite their poverty and adverse conditions.

Second Response

When the suicide rate in America is as high as it is, and rising steadily,
I can't imagine how bad it must be in the ghettos of South Africa.

Prayer of a South African Jewish Father
by Greg Thayer
(Journal. *Somehow Tenderness Survives,* "A Day in the Country")

O Lord, give me the strength to stand up for what is right,
and to help the downtrodden, and to not be afraid of what
others may think or to be ashamed of what I do for you.

Chapter 5

The Pathway to Darkness
The Holocaust

Lynda Miller

Mary Greenberg

Teachers learn a great deal from parents. Mary Greenberg is a parent and she is also a poet. The following is one of her poems.

It's in the Picture

For so long I thought you ill
Joy nor contentment had your attention.

But this is something I overlooked.
This sign of triumph, strength.
Why else is this photo by your side?

They found you broken but alive.
Not wasting time, you started at renewing life.
Food, shelter, clothing, you thought you needed these the most.
But memories ... memories were pushed aside.

Except those garbs of death.
Why put them on again?
"Who would believe me, otherwise?"

See me.
Your new strong self.
Your billfold picture shows your face clean, not wasted.
Your smile triumphant, not pained.
Those clothes remain; the stripes of death you overcame.

Yes, you survived.
This image is a testament to it.

But to this day I realize,
Your heart did not.

Mary Greenberg's father had been a young man in Greece at the start of World War II. When he was younger his parents were able to send him to France for part of his education. While there, he learned to speak French, something which was to prove invaluable to him later on. As the war progressed, and Greece became occupied by Nazi troops, Mary's father and his family found themselves, their friends, neighbors, and acquaintances in grave danger. Eventually all but five percent of the Jewish population of Greece was to perish under Hitler's domination. Mary's father was one of the five percent who survived. He thought this was probably because he could speak French. Mary explained that Hitler's "final solution" was more successful in Greece than anywhere else in Europe because few Greeks understood German or French and as a result could not follow SS soldiers orders quickly enough. Many were simply shot as they stood not knowing what was expected of them or what was being done to themselves or their families. However, because her father understood French, he was helped by the Jews from France who told him what to do to possibly survive in the midst of mass murder. Yet by the time Mary's father was "liberated" virtually his entire family had been murdered. He was the only one to survive.

Mary explained that this had a profound impact on whom she had become. The Holocaust was never spoken of as she grew up. And for a long time she didn't understand the sense of profound melancholy and dread felt by her father. She loved him. She wanted to please him and to make him happy. But his heart had been broken long before she existed and there was nothing anyone could do. But Mary didn't know this. She only knew that while other children spoke of aunts and uncles and grandparents for her there were none. It was as if her father had sprung forth on his own as a full grown adult. These things haunted Mary, just as surely as the pain of what had happened to himself and his family haunted her father.

Later, when she was an adult, and the painful secret had slowly, piece by piece been revealed to her, she realized that the devastation of the Holocaust had not ended with the liberation of the death camps. And that the grief and fear had only begun. She realized that she was a child of that grief and fear. Mary was determined that her children or grandchildren would not become the future victims of the Holocaust.

Two years later, the focus of our Ethnic Week library forums was the Holocaust. Mary Greenberg was invited by Diane Goheen and Mike Printz to be one of our featured speakers and she helped to organize this study.

Teachers learn a great deal from parents. We learned from Mary Greenberg that there is tragically, no way in the last half of the twentieth century to understand modern Judaism or the twentieth century Jewish faith without first confronting the Holocaust. It has left western civilization scarred and shamed as one of our great civilized nations systematically destroyed people simply because they were of the Jewish faith. It would be better if we did not have to teach this at all. Better of course, if the tragedy had never occurred. However, just as Apartheid exists and is painful to realize, just as once African American citizens were enslaved and then kept from their constitutional rights, just as the Native American was cheated and dehumanized, the Holocaust happened. And we would be wrong if we did not include in any multicultural curriculum a look at this tragedy, however difficult it may be for us to do so. To prevent future Holocausts—to become aware of the fact that this could (and in fact has occurred in varying degree) on our own soil—we must realize what happened. And to empathize with victims of the Holocaust, we must teach about the Holocaust.

Language Arts Activities for a Study of the Holocaust

Literature Base: *Auschwitz: True Tales from a Grotesque Land,* by Sara Nomberg Przytyk. Translated by Roslyn Hirsch. *Night,* by Elie Wiesel.

These two books are powerfully written documentations of what occurred in what is considered the worst of the Nazi death camps in World War II. Taught together as a unit they present two perspectives on the same experience. Wiesel recalls his experience as a fifteen-year-old boy robbed not only of his family, but also his faith in God and humanity. Nomberg Przytyk writes from experiences that occurred at the same place and time, but from the perspective of an adult, politically active young woman who somehow manages to observe the very worst in human behavior and still retain her belief in herself. She bears not only witness to the evil of Auschwitz but to those who attained greatness in their compassion and dignity of spirit. One of these books is no less important or poignant or powerfully written than the other. Together they speak to what we may become if we forget our humanity. Because of the advanced vocabulary, and graphic images portrayed within these books, they are most suited for students in grades nine through twelve.

Procedures and Activities

Because these books are so closely related in content, students read both in their entirety, beginning with *Night*. We started with *Night* because Wiesel is writing about something which occurred at the point in his life when he was the same age as the students. He is fifteen at the start of the book. My students in freshman and sophomore English are fourteen and fifteen years old. As students completed this reading, they used a reading journal which is specifically tailored for this book.

The Reading Journal: *Letters from the Holocaust*

To complete their reading journal, students empathized with the Wiesel family as it is portrayed in Elie Wiesel's biographical account, *Night*. To do this, they looked at the characters of the family and began their journal by writing a letter in the voice of one of the family members. They selected three points in the book and wrote three different letters from that character to Elie Wiesel (the author of the book and the eldest son of the Wiesel family). The following is a copy of the letter assignment provided to students (see Chapter 6 for student exemplars):

> Pretend that you are one of the following characters from *Night* and write three letters to Elie Wiesel as if you *are* that character. Try to empathize as much as possible. Select three points within the story, and write what is going on at that moment in your life (as that character). You will be evaluated on how well you are able to capture the plight and imagined voice of this character. You may choose to be Moshe the Beadle, Mrs. Wiesel, Eli's baby sister Tzipora, or Eli's father the elder Wiesel.
>
> Write each of these three letters from different points in time. Once from a point in time before the Jewish people of Sighet were transferred into a ghetto; once during the time they were placed in the ghetto and once from a point in time before the war has ended and most of the population has died or is imprisoned at Auschwitz or Birkenau or Buna.

This assignment provides some very poignant letters and comments from the students. On the day the letters are due, students are formed into groups of four to five and read their letters aloud to one another. One letter is selected from each student. Then the letters are compiled into a booklet of Holocaust writings which is intended as a way to share students voices and experiences of this book with others outside of the class.

To continue our study, students were assigned writings to be completed as they read *Auschwitz: True Tales from a Grotesque Land*. This book is gripping and it is particularly powerful in bringing to life the personalities of the women who populated the devastation that was Auschwitz. Because of this, students focused upon the characterization within the book. They were required to select one character depicted within the book and write in the voice of that character as she once was before Auschwitz and as she is after Auschwitz. This writing was eventually worked into a poem which is a monologue between the given character as she was and as she comes to be within the book. The following is the assignment I give to my students. (See Chapter 6 for student exemplars.)

> Select a character from the book *Auschwitz: True Tales from a Grotesque Land* and write a dialogue in which the character speaks on one side of the page as she was *before* Auschwitz and on the other side of the page as she was *after* Auschwitz. On the day this writing is due, you will meet in a writing workshop in which you will decide which words, phrases and their arrangement will work best in creating a poem from this assignment. You will then have three days to complete a finished, publishable poem. The following poem was written by art instructor Lynda Miller as part of her participation in this activity.

> My fairy tales and dreams fade and all hope becomes a void.
> All sandwiched up between barbed wire walls and gates
> with no passages out. I wear numbers for my name
> And loneliness in my heart. It is so cold.
>   I am so alone in a crowd.
> Each day is an eternity filled with doubt. A sense of loss.
> Hunger, and pain. There are ears always listening and
> Eyes always watching ... Watching. I have no place to go.
>   I must be strong.
> Fear is everywhere ... Fear is deep inside of me and
> Worn well on other faces, of ages I will never reach.
> I have no place to hide.
>   I'm afraid to cry.
>   I wonder why...

Why am I so different?
Why must I die?

These poems are then published in the same booklet as the letters.

Literature Base: *Number the Stars*, by Lois Lowry

While *Auschwitz: True Tales from a Grotesque Land* and *Night* are invaluable nonfiction first-hand accounts of the horror of the Holocaust, *Number the Stars* is a poignant, powerful young adult fiction book. It is a tale of heroism, courage, and friendship set against the threat of the Nazi regime and its invasion into Denmark. *Number the Stars* is a book written with the young adult audience in mind, and because of this it is easily read by students from seventh through twelfth grades. Yet, do not let the fact that this book is intended for a young audience stop you from using it at the senior high level. *Number the Stars* is a well-told tale and can be used to teach even the most advanced high school student.

As Lowry accurately describes in her afterword, Denmark was unique among the countries that were invaded by the Germans during World War II. Denmark managed to hide most of its Jewish citizens for the duration of the Nazi occupation and in the process very few Jewish Danes suffered the Nazi death campus or died as a result of the Holocaust. Lowry's story is a historical novel of one family's successful rescue of their neighbors and friends. The protagonist is a ten-year-old little girl, Annemarie, who must exhibit extraordinary courage in order to help in the rescue of her best friend Ellen and Ellen's family. The character of Annemarie and the Nazi occupation of Denmark provide lessons in the literary heroine.

Students begin this study by defining what a hero is. After they wrote their definitions, they read newspaper clippings which depict heroic deeds performed by ordinary citizens. The class once again was divided into groups and students discussed within these groups their respective articles. They then select one which they feel represents the greatest act of heroism and following this (which takes about forty-five minutes) one person from each group explains the article they chose, why they chose it and how it particularly represents heroism. Following this class period, students were taught about the classic hero. The classic hero exhibits the following attributes.

1. Extraordinary birth or circumstances which are beyond his/her control at a very young age.

2. A type of divine intervention or extraordinary luck in survival and triumph.

3. An inordinate degree of personal courage or integrity.

4. A tendency to put personal needs aside for the greater good of their society.

Students wrote reading journals in which they describe how Annemarie and her family meet the criteria of the classic hero (see Chapter 6 for student exemplars). They also wrote in the same journal why such heroes (fictional and real) are necessary as role models for us. In other words, students wrote what such characters have to teach us. From this journal, students completed a formal essay in which they go on to describe why Annemarie (or one of the other characters in this book) is in fact heroic. Students then research a person who is currently living and who they feel meets the criteria for the classic hero. They are asked to research this person and write an essay in which they describe and define why this particular individual may be a role model in heroism for the rest of us. Students are allowed a total of two weeks to complete this assignment. Two class periods are spent doing library research.

Literature Base: *Manzanar*, by John Armor and Peter Wright.

During the same time Auschwitz was functioning to exterminate the Jews of Europe, and the Annemaries of Denmark were saving their neighbors' lives, over 110,000 men, women, and children of Japanese descent were sent to concentration camps in the United States. More than 10,000 of them ended up in Manzanar a "relocation center" in the California desert. The people of Manzanar and the camp itself were photographed by Ansel Adams, and were the subjects of his only photo-journalistic effort. He donated the photographs to the Library of Congress and they were not seen for forty-five years. However, they may be seen in the pages of this book which also includes an essay by John Hersey that documents what happened to our Japanese citizens during the period after the attack on Pearl Harbor until the end of World War II. Because it portrays a tragedy brought about by the injustice and attitude of our own government and people during the same time period as the Holocaust, it may enhance an understanding of the Holocaust in a way no other book can.

After reading accounts of the German Holocaust this book is particu-larly chilling. Here in our own country American citizens were robbed of their homes, placed behind barbed wire, and made to live in the most adverse of conditions. According to John Hersey's account: "Conditions at Manzanar were harsh. Even in the late spring, the nighttime temperatures in the valley dropped to freezing. In summer, temperatures often rose above 110 degrees. Despite the climate, the prisoners were required to grow their own food." Coupled with this stark account are Ansel Adams photographs. Unrelenting in their clarity and beauty we see face after face looking out at us from time and reminding us of what may happen again if we don't pay attention.

Because the images in this book are so beautiful and speak so clearly about the character of the Japanese who were interned at Manzanar, students focused upon what they are able to discern form the photographs by Ansel Adams. While the account is important, and students are required to read at least part of it in order to gain a complete understanding of what the photographs portray, the major emphasis in a study of this book is the illustrations (see Chapter 6 for student work). The following is the assignment given to students (adapted in part from the book *Getting from Here to There: Writing and Reading Poetry*, by Florence Grossman, Boyton/Cook, 1982, p. 95).

Look through the photographs in the book *Manzanar* and study the faces, the clothing. Are the people in the photograph posing or were they interrupted in the middle in something when the photograph was taken? What are they saying? What would they say to their counterparts in Europe, the victims of the Holocaust? How do you imagine their lives at the moment Ansel Adams took the picture?

Choose the photo that most captures your imagination and using your imagination walk into it, look out of it. Write a poem that will make us see the photo and beyond the photo. Make the words more than the picture. Make the picture speak to us of Manazar through your words.

Art Activities for the Holocaust

Literature Base: *Auschwitz: True Tales from a Grotesque Land*, by Sara Normberg-Przytyk.

With the study of the Holocaust, the art department actively involved our independent study students with this program. These students were selected to participate because of the nature of the subject matter and the difficulty of the assignment. The students were assigned to work with me on a one-to-one basis. They all were visually advanced and were assigned projects in the area of drawing and printmaking.

The art assignments for our Holocaust study were divided up into four parts: research, sketchbook, reference to art history, and finished work. The students were to first, involve themselves with the literature selected for our study. As the students did their research, they kept a sketchbook of information to record visual images as well as important names, dates and places that seemed significant to them as they grasped an understanding of the brutality and suffering of the Jewish people during the Holocaust.

Their sketchbooks were also used to record information gained by studying art history. They were asked to view four specific works of art to determine how noted artists historically have recorded the injustices of man, war, and human suffering.

For this assignment, the students were to look up Francisco Goya's, "The Third of May, 1808." This painting by Goya depicts the brutality and suffering caused by war. To Goya, war meant only death and destruction, and he used his art to pass his feelings on to others.

The second artist that the students were asked to research was Edvard Munch, whose entire life was marked with tragedy and pain (both emotional and physical). The selected work from Edvard Munch was "The Scream," because of its emotional impact. The artist's message was to show the observer what it would look like to live in a world of anguish.

"Death of the Mother," by Kathe Kollwitz, was the third work of art for the students to research. It was created to demonstrate the terrifying struggle of a mother trying to protect her child from death. Kathe Kollwitz was a German Expressionists who used her art to protest against the tragic plight of the poor before and after World War I.

Pablo Picasso was the fourth artist that the students had to study during their Holocaust unit. The specific work by Pablo Picasso that we studied was "Guernica." This work was completed in 1937 as a reaction to the bombing of the ancient Spanish city of Guernica during the Spanish Civil War. In this work, Picasso wanted to show the horrors and agony, and the waste of modern warfare.

The fourth part of their assignment was to develop a finished drawing or printmaking project that depicted a person expressing some aspect of human emotion. Our past cultural study asked the students to try to learn about others and depict the elements of their society that demonstrated an understanding of that culture. This Holocaust study was designed to teach understanding. However, the intent was to also teach these young artists how art forms have historically been created to teach a message to the masses. Artists by nature have historically recorded man's inhumanity to man, human suffering that occurs during war, the emotional pain of the loss of a loved one, and social or political injustices during their lifetimes. The students were to depict a human face that represented the losses to all of humanity through the injustices and brutality that took place during the Holocaust. They could vary their approach by depicting the faces of the victims, the faces of those who lost love ones, the faces of those who implemented these injustices, or develop a portraiture of the masses of people who stood by and let it happen. They could also develop a face which could be used as a reminder of the Holocaust to serve as a message to our masses of people today. They could depict faces of war or battle. They were told that they could even use their own face as a sounding board for their feelings about the Holocaust. The students were invited to read *Number the Stars* by Lois Lowry and depict the face of a silent hero.

Students worked approximately three weeks on this project and received a grade on their sketchbook as well as their finished art project. Their work was matted and placed on display during the library forums as well as into their portfolio for competition during the remaining part of the school year.

The students created universal messages that we are all victims of war, suffering, and human injustices inflicted upon us by other men in the name of superiority. The students learned to use emotion within their work to express personal opinions. They were not asked to do creative writing for sharing their readings about the Holocaust, however, they did include many brief writings in their sketchbook. These projects were successful and gave the viewer an insight into both the artists and their messages.

Chapter 6
Illuminating the Pathway
Into the Night

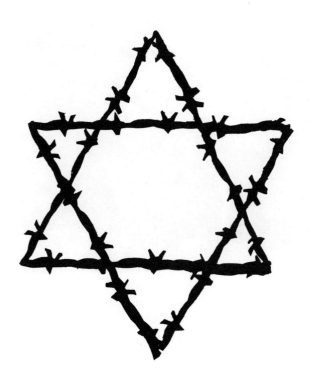

Scott Ramser, Linoleum print

Orli
by Melissa Shivers
(Character Poem. *Auschwitz: True Tales from a Grotesque Land*)

A long time ago, in 1933 Orli was taken
  by Hitler's rule through the gates of
  Auschwitz
She was a loyal young woman
  She believed in her country.
Involvement in the manifesto stole her
  life away
A brave woman who had the courage of a lion
  She was all she could be to the other
  inmates.
Her strong compassion kept her
  on top,
  and left others behind.
The power of leadership allowed
  her to play god
  with the lives of many women
  in her same position
The fight for life made her a cruel,
  cold-hearted roller coaster.
Her understanding ways saved
  the lives of some chosen ones
  on the death block.
Yet those cold cold-hearted hands beat
  the innocent, starving human beings
  at will.
The horror and trauma of survival
  made her a tyrant,
  and a savior
  for all who crossed her path.

Upon Leaving the Budhist Church
by Jennifer Zibell
(Based on Photograph. *Manzanar*)

past this white sky
these black skeletons freeze
into their pose
they'll live longer
than me
they'll be here
the snow gives the desert
a proper change of clothes
virgin white snow
hides the bleeding sore
that is my existence
while I search the reasons
why all I see is the clarity
it is an
insolent snow of regret
deserting me, here
until I prove
like the blackened trees
that I have been choked
but it only takes one spring
of prosperity
to show you are wrong
I live

Emily Eakes, Monoprint

Mary Nall, Monoprint

Letters from *Night*
by Katharine Humphrey
(Letter Journal Assignment. *Night*)

My Dear Friend Eliezer,

I am writing you this letter to try to warn you of what I know is to come. I have told my stories to try to warn our people but they think me mad. You are my last hope Eliezer, so I will tell my story to you one last time and hope you believe.

When we were deported, we were not taken to work in Galicia as you have heard. Instead, we were taken into a forest, made to dig our own graves, and then mercilessly shot, one at a time. Even the babies, Eliezer. Worse is to come for you and the rest of our people. I know for I have asked God and felt his answer. You must convince as many people of the truth of my tale as you can and then you must leave. Go far away where Hitler's monsters cannot reach you.

You have heard my tales just as everyone else has. Now I ask you simply to believe in them and run far away from here, alone if you must. I will pray for you and all our people daily.

> May God be with you, Eliezer,
> Mosche the Beadle

Eliezer,

I am writing you again to try to warn you one last time to get far away from here, but I am afraid that I am too late. Already our people are being held prisoner in the ghettos. I have been in this position before and I know what you are thinking. You have probably heard that we are to be taken to factories to work. This is a lie. We are to be taken to die. I also know that where we are to be taken will be worse than where I was taken the first time. I cannot explain how I know this, perhaps God has seen fit to put all our faith in Him, and trust our lives to Him. Above all we must not lose our faith, for besides each other that is all we have. Do not lose your faith in God and He will be with you. I hope you will survive what is to come, in body as well as spirit.

> Mosche the Beadle

Eliezer,

I write you this letter not knowing if you are alive or dead. Most probably you have died, so many have that I have no reason to believe you are alive. If indeed you do survive, I can not say that you are among the lucky, but if you do perhaps one day this will reach you.

I tried to warn you, I tried to warn all of you. Now you see that I was right. Oh how I wish that I wasn't. My worst fears for our people have been realized in places like Buna, Auschwitz, and Birkenau. But I stray from my purpose. I am writing this letter to ask one last favor from you and I know that you will see the importance of this one. I myself would do it but I know I will not survive another selection.

The horrors of these places that we have been will haunt and terrify you forever, but if you survive, no matter how much you want to you must never forget them. This is the favor that I ask of you, not to forget, to tell your story. Tell it to anyone and everyone. Write about it, do anything but forget it. In order to keep another Holocaust like this one from ever happening again you and the rest of the survivors must make sure that people know about it and all its horrors and never forget. This is the favor that I ask of you Eliezer. I know it will be hard but it must be done.

I must go now. God is waiting for me. I have so many questions to ask of Him and perhaps I will begin to understand the answers. So many questions....

Do not forget Eliezer. Whatever you do, do not ever forget, for the moment you do it will happen again.

Mosche the Beadle

Journal
by Jenny Moerer
(Hero Journal. *Number the Stars*)

Not only is the protagonist, Annemarie, of *Number the Stars* a classic hero, but likewise are her family and friends.

Beyond her own control, Annemarie spends a great amount of her childhood in the midst of the Holocaust. Thus, not only is Annemarie exposed to grueling acts against innocent people, but she is exposed and greatly influenced by the giving, sharing, and selflessness of her friends and family. Annemarie is influenced by these noble traits such that they are the traits by which she acts when her friends are in danger.

Annemarie is blessed with luck in many of her encounters with the soldiers, particularly when she stopped with the handkerchief. The lives of many, including her own, are saved partially due to the luck with which she is blessed along the way to her uncle's boat. Additionally, Annemarie's bravery and wit lead her to success in helping her friends to Sweden. This act enhances Annemarie's selflessness and integrity. She puts the needs of others before her own. A strong example of this is when at an early age, Annemarie proudly states that she would be the King's bodyguard; she would die for her country. As one can easily deduce, Annemarie fits the criteria for the classic hero as well as the criteria for a good person.

Characters like Annemarie, heroes, are vital for the human spirit. Whether a prince or serf, a hero is appealing to us. It seems the heroic one is looked upon by others as having integrity and bravery. Because these are highly sought after traits, we may model our lives after these good people. In nearly every account of a classic hero, a lesson is to be learned. *Number the Stars* teaches us that at tragic times, selfless love is the key to bravery and that bravery is not something that only fairy tale characters can possess, but real people can as well. Heroes point out the good things in us and provoke us to make the choice of what kind of person we are going to be. Heroes are selfless, and if we model ourselves after them, the selflessness will greatly help society as a whole. Heroes in books like Annemarie are necessary to show us how to maintain the good of the human spirit.

Victim
by Rachael Chan
(Short Story)
Instructor: Ann Elmborg

She was oblivious to the writing on the wall. Her eyes sunk deep into her head as fatigue washed over her body. Her mind moved with gears and switches as she pulled the lifeless bags into the darkened service hallway toward the trash room. She slunk down the hall, avoiding stranger's eyes. "Hi," the eyes spoke. "Tired?" And yet his voice trailed off as if the word had taken his last breath. A nod and she disappeared through the door, the bags following close on her heels.

Not surprisingly, the eyes were still there when she emerged from the stench filled room; a throbbing pain pulsing through her shoulder. She winced.

"So," the eyes lurched, "when do you, ah, get off?"

A strong, fermented smell filled her nostrils and her heart began pounding harder and faster. Suddenly, there was nothing else but her and the eyes—her and the eyes. They grew closer and closer, twitching back and forth. Red lightning shot through them. She stepped back—no, was pushed back—hard against the stone like wall. Her muscles gave out as if a magnetic force was trying to pull her limp body through the solid wall. Pain raced through her. Her eyes, big and round, saw nothing but the hate of the eyes forcing her head back further and further. The pungent, fermented smell now dripped into her mouth. A pale cast fell over her eyes like a blanket, her head throbbing; blackness ceased her terror.

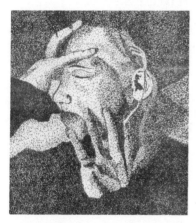

Rachael Chan, Pen and Ink
Instructor: Ann Elmborg

Shell
by Jennifer Zibell
(Found Poem. *Auschwitz: True Tales From a Grotesque Land*)
Instructor: Doug Goheen

I am not human.
I am a shell of what I was.
Food is good.
Sleep is good.
But what am I worth?
Not even half a ration.
A gray, blank mind,

Like the smoke seeping out of the crematorium,
Like a part of my soul seeps out
Into darkness, brightened by flesh flames.
No soldier, I don't want you to go to the gas for me,
I'm wondering how you can sleep at night.
Oh, it all used to bother me:
The pain, fear, suspense, pressure, suffering.
For now, give me my ration—
A little thin soup, a slice of bread.
Selection tomorrow, do I worry or care?
I am only a shell of what I could have been.
So if I go to the gas,
Only a part of me will die,
My soul has long been extinguished.

Blood and Tears
by John Blosser
(Free Verse. *Auswitchz: True Tales from a Grotesque Land*)

Mother, my mother,
cannot comfort me anymore.
Just another dirty Jew—
        Hungarian, Greek, German, Danish, Polish,
She was taken to the showers which bore
        faucets raining blood and tears,
as soon as we arrived.
She is not here anymore,
only her ashes remain,
so I must continue on—
        head shaven, chest sunken, and belly bloated,
with but a dim flicker of hope in my sapient eyes.
Death is looming closer with the unwavering arrival
of flocks upon flocks of naive Zugangen.
        And, as the camp continues to crowd,
        I fear
                I am destined to be
                        but another victim of this
                                brutal
                                        genocide.

Tracie Niles, Calliograph

One Good Man
by Spencer Duncan
(Classic Hero Essay. *Number the Stars*)

There are those who believe that persons of all faiths, cultures, creeds, and beliefs should be able to live together equally. However, these beliefs are held and acted on by very few people, but there is still hope. There are people out there who hold these beliefs and act on them; that is why we notice these people. One of these individuals is Father Richard Etzel. According to a 1990 video oral history interview conducted by Topeka West High School students, as a boy Father Etzel did some brief moving around between different churches and several schools. When he became a priest, he was sent to St. Mary's Church in Kansas City, Kansas. Here Father Etzel made a decision to help those less fortunate. He began the St. Mary's food kitchen. After improving the St. Mary's kitchen, he was sent to Topeka. There he helped begin a program that is taking homeless families off the street.

Father Etzel said in the 1990 video oral history interview that all people deserve the necessities of life and that no person should have to live on the streets. The Topeka Family Shelter, Inc. was born out of that conviction. The shelter was patterned after a program in Liberty, Missouri. The theme of the program is not to just house the homeless, but to enable the homeless, through education in budgeting, homemaking, nutrition, community living, job enhancement, economic independence and emotional self-confidence, to become independent. Up to twenty or more homeless families receive these services ninety days free. They also receive an apartment free of charge for ninety days. After that time the shelter still aids the family in finding a job. The program not only has a high success rate, but it is addressing both the immediate housing crisis and the underlying causes. This program is making the community more aware of the homeless problem and forcing the community to begin to do something about it. Most of all this program helps people get a sense of self-esteem and gives them a chance to feel hope about the future, and takes them off the street.

Father Etzel has instilled emotional confidence in the homeless families that he has helped. He has given these people the ability to once again stand on their own feet in society and stay there. Father Etzel's struggle is to guarantee that every man, woman, and child has access to shelter, food, education, and job opportunity. He has created an awareness in the community of the plight of the homeless and because of this awareness the community has been forced to acknowledge the homeless. Through Father Etzel's peaceful fight for the rights of the homeless, another issue has been brought to light. That issue is public housing. Father Etzel has worked for affordable housing that is decent and that will be offered to all.

He believes that the homeless are people who are just down on their luck, and is willing to do what it takes to help his people gain economic independence. Father Etzel struggles with the conditions of poverty and the selfish and apathetic people who refuse to help the homeless. He has succeeded in bringing attention to the needs of the homeless in Topeka and creating for them an opportunity for a better life. He is a hero who uses courage, nonviolence, and truth to bring about justice.

Chapter 7
The Circle at the End of the Path
Native American

Shawn Miller. Pen and Ink

Dennis Rogers

To study the Native American is to study ourselves. This was made abundantly clear to us when, as part of the Ethnic Week activities for this unit, a Native American Holy Man came to my creative writing class and told my students about himself and his beliefs. He was a Kickapoo Indian and lived on a reservation about seventy miles north of our school on Highway 75. When asked how he felt about "white" America he stated: "You may not appreciate or realize it—but to live here, to walk on this land, see these skies, hear the voices of the animals who make this place their home is to be at least in part Indian. You are nurtured by the same hills and waters and your spirit drinks from the same beauty first seen by Indians. It does not matter if your grandparents came from Germany or Africa or China. How can you not be at least in part Indian? It is impossible." And so our study of the Native American would become a study of our own past and present.

No matter where you are in America, the Kickapoo Holy Man was right: you are, by virtue of walking this landscape of America, at least in part Native American. We began our study of the Native American with sand painting. Dennis Rogers, an employee in our school district and a Navajo, offered to demonstrate this art by completing a sand painting in the Library for art, creative writing, and mythology classes.

Dennis arrived promptly at 9:00 A.M. He was wearing a beautiful hand trimmed red shirt, turquoise jewelry, and a small intricately beaded head band. He is five-foot six, slightly built and he moves and speaks quietly. Yet, in spite of his small stature and quiet attitude, he held the greatest presence in the room. He immediately went about his task. He began by dumping a pile of ash white sand on a large table. He then patted it into a perfect circle using a rhythmic pattern. His fingers danced over the sand and it yielded, creating a fine circular white canvas. He next took ten small plastic containers out of a cardboard box. Each one held a different brilliant color: fiery orange, pitch black, deep purple, brilliant shades of reds and turquoise, and subtle blues and browns.

At that point, one of the students asked if Dennis had somehow dyed the sand. He explained that he did not dye the sand, but that he had "captured" it by rubbing together stones he collected from the Painted Desert during the summer. Another student asked who had taught him sand painting. He answered that no one had taught him. His father had been a chief and medicine man who had practiced the art. Dennis recounted how as a small child he would watch as his father worked. One day his father simply handed over a collection of rocks and sand and told Dennis, "This is what you should do." After telling us all this, he began to paint.

He closed his eyes and carefully moved to pick up some black sand. He held it in his palm and, using his thumb as a "brush" with the most careful, gentle motions, began to place the sand on his "canvas." As he did, he explained that he was not sure what the painting would become. He hesitated and then went on to say that the painting would have a life of its own and when it was finished, he would tell its meaning. We watched in silence as Dennis formed hair, a face, feathers, a dress, moccasins, and finally a lightning bolt all of sand on sand. We watched as the sand did indeed form a life of its own in the intricacy of the work itself. The hair flowed: the skirt was rawhide. In the maiden's hand was the lightning bolt of bright yellow pointing toward a blue heaven.

Dennis finished and then explained that the painting was a prayer. In this case, he knew that the prayer should be a request for rain. That was what the lightning bolt meant and that was why he had chosen a female figure. He also told us that, because the painting was only sand on sand, it was not permanent but even so it was sacred and would have to be taken apart in a prescribed manner. He said he would leave it for the students to enjoy that afternoon and that he would come to remove it on Friday. It was Wednesday. It rained that afternoon and for the next two days. Never have we experienced a more enthusiastically received introduction to a unit of study. And through allowing students to interact personally with the Navajo culture, we provided them with an experience that would enhance their understanding of the art of sand painting, the mythology of the Navajo, and the character of the modern Navajo.

Language Arts Activities for a Study of Native American Indians

Literature Base: *Words in the Blood: Contemporary Indian Writers of North and South America*, by Jamake Highwater

Dennis's visit did provide students with something that every writer of fiction seeks: a model for character development. The creative writing students were required to write a short story. However, short stories are very difficult assignments for the novice (or even experienced) writer. It was important for students to read, meet, and experience as much Native American culture as possible in order to successfully write a story in which the characters were Native Americans.

The book provided for Ethnic Week, "An Awareness of Native Americans," *Words in the Blood: Contemporary Indian Writers of North and South America,* proved to be an excellent resource for my students. It contains poetry, short stories, and essays which are among the best in American Literature and certainly representative of the best in Native American Literature. It is also a book which reaches students with poetry and prose which may be appreciated (depending upon the selection) at every level from seventh through twelfth grades. However, students only had access to this book for one week. Students focused on a particular section of the book, and depending on whether they were working on a short story or poetry, based what they studied from the book upon what they would be writing. The following books were also available to students throughout our study of this unit:

Allen, Paula Gunn. *Spider Woman's Granddaughters: Traditional Tales and Contemporary Writing by Native American Women.* New York: Fawcett Columbine, 1989.

Debo, Angie. *A History of the Indians of the United States.* University of Oklahoma Press, 1983.

Erdoes, Richard, and Alfonso Ortiz. *American Indian Myths and Legends.* New York: Pantheon Books, 1984.

Hamilton, Charles. *Cry of the Thunderbird: The American Indian's Own Story.* Norman, OK, University of Oklahoma Press, 1989.

Silko, Leslie Marmon. *Storyteller.* New York: Arcade Publishing, 1981.

Each book provided some insight into a particular aspect of Native American culture or literature. Students read aloud from *Storyteller,* told myths from *American Indian Myths and Legends,* and gleaned information on the history of the Indian from *Cry of the Thunderbird* and *A History of the Indians of the United States. Spider Woman's Granddaughters* proved a valuable source (along with *Words in the Blood*) of stories by Native Americans about Native Americans.

Procedures and Activities

The Short Story

Students who were writing short stories based upon a Native American protagonist needed to have great understanding and empathy for their character. One student, Greg Thayer, was particularly successful in writing a short story and creating a believable protagonist. He began by writing a summary of the story he was intending to write. In other words, he wrote what was going to happen to his protagonist before he "fleshed out" his character with details and background information. Once he had done this he brought his idea (which was written out) to class for workshopping in a group with four other student writers and myself. After bringing his first writing to this workshop he decided that he needed to develop the following in order to complete his story.

1. A personal history for his protagonist.
2. A history of the other characters within the story (in this case the protagonist's parents) who interact in a significant way with the protagonist.
3. Research of the mythology and beliefs presented in the story.
4. Research on the setting in which the story takes place.

Greg went through several revisions of his story before he was satisfied, but he feels now that the research he completed and the study of the Native American culture was important to his successful completion of this story.

Prior to ever beginning this unit, students had been taught the elements of a short story, and understood that in order to have a short story which is a story the following elements must be present.

1. A protagonist who is going to meet a challenge which will cause him or her success or failure.
2. An antagonist who is an equal match for the protagonist.
3. Complications which are going to build suspense and make the reader wonder whether or not the protagonist is going to succeed in meeting the challenge.
4. A crisis moment in the story in which the reader knows what the outcome for the protagonist will be.
5. Resolution, that part of the story in which all the "loose ends" are tied up and questions are answered.

Greg's story is particularly sophisticated in addressing these elements. It reflects his empathy for his Native American protagonist and the care he took in completing his research. See Chapter 8 for Greg Thayer's story, "The Scream of the Hawk."

Character Poetry

A poetry assignment which lends itself to interpretation of literature in *Words in the Blood* and also explores characterization, is a variation on the Found Poem. (See Chapter 3.) In this poetry assignment, students are asked to locate words and phrases from a story which particularly reveal the personality, feelings, goals and problems of a given character. In other words, those precise words which when isolated and manipulated into a poem will give us the greatest insight into who a character is. We should know more about the character reading the poem than we would simply reading the book from which the poem was taken.

Students should watch for these things when looking for the words and phrases within a work of literature for use in this poem: distinctive gestures; secret thoughts only the character knows; a scene in which the character is alone with his or her thoughts; words or phrases which reveal the physical appearance of a given character. The idea is to bring the character to life in a way that isn't possible in conventional prose writing.

Chant/Song Poetry

The section "The Cantares Mexicanos, Five Songs and a Fragment" in *Words in the Blood* provides inspiration for this assignment. A chant poem has no traditional form, but it is a poem in which one or more lines are repeated over and over. It is meant to be read or recited aloud usually by more than one person. This type of poetry dates back to a time when people would sit around a fire after the sunset and tell stories and invoke magical spells and incantations to protect themselves from wild animals, storms, or drought. This also might be a way of asking for a good hunt or to have lots of healthy children. The chant could also be a lament for something lost.

A chant depends upon the repetition of words and phrases over and over again in a rhythm. Chant poetry is driven by its beat. After reading the poetry from this section of *Words in the Blood*, students should try to write their own by first deciding what they want to chant about and then coming up with a good line that makes a statement and lends itself well to repetition. Here is a sample of a chant the teachers wrote to model this assignment about the Kickapoo tribe trying to obtain a license for a Casino to be operated on their reservation near Holton, Kansas.

The Kansa first walked this prairie.
Our great grandfathers' fathers,
Over the land that stretched to
The setting sun
The Great fathers of this Kansas Land

Their gamble—drought and hunger
Their only fear—the buffalo would move
To greener pastures
They did not know what would become
Of their children
The Great Fathers of this Kansas Land

They would question our need for casinos
What does Lady Luck have to do with Mother Earth?
We are the children of the Kansa and this Kansas Land
Do we not have the same big sky?
The same rains? The same grasses?
The Great Fathers' questions

Are sacred circles roulette wheels?
All fathers' question

The buffalo are no more
The white man gambled and we lost
Fences and roads cut the earth
Answers for our Great Fathers
Answers for all fathers

To hold the riches of this Kansas Land
We look to Lady Luck
And pray for a wild card
A gamble we hope not to lose
Answers for our Great Fathers

Namesakes of this Kansas Land
Our Great Fathers
Be at rest
We hear you still
In this North Wind
In this Prairie Sky
This Prairie Earth
Our fathers' prayer
Our Great Fathers' answer

Poems of Nature

To be Native American is to be in tune with the natural environment. It is to treat all living creatures with a deep respect and wonder. Many of the poems in *Word in the Blood* reflect the high regard and empathy Native Americans feel for all life on earth. Students enjoy getting outside to do writing assignments and if they focus their attention, students write poetry that reflects the beauty of their own natural environment. The following is an outdoor poetry assignment (see Chapter 8 for student exemplars).

For one hour become a Native American. Look at the land and the natural surroundings in Topeka with the respect the Native American does. Find a place outside where you can sit and write what you see. One of the problems in writing about the natural world is the tendency to become trite and to use cliches (words that have been so overused by so many people that they no longer mean very much). But if you become Native American, you will be able to look at something individually. As you write about an object think about what it might feel, what would it say if it could talk? What does it know? What threatens it? Is this flower or leaf or rock familiar to you or a stranger? Does it have a soft personality? Is it sweet in temperament or angry? What does it remind you of? A childhood moment? Someone you know? Put this into your writing as you sit and contemplate the object you've chosen.

When you are satisfied you have written everything you can think of about your subject, move on to another flower, or leaf, or stone until you have written for at least twenty minutes.

When we return to the classroom, you will have one class period
to write your poem, one class period to workshop your poem,
and one class period to decide how you want to visually present
your poem.

This assignment may become part of a class field trip to a nearby park.
We went to Shunga Park near our high school where I completed this poem
as part of this assignment.

Shunga Creek

The sun filters
 through a lace of life
 formed by the trees
 that were here twenty-five years
 ago when Phillip
 carried a small child
 across the creek

Bullhead could be caught
 in a mother's borrowed colander
 even the leeches were a fascination

The leaves of last autumn rustle
 above a lavender flower
 a five point star

The same flower picked by
 a child of ten
 (to appease the mother for having fished with colander)

The child did not know what
 to call the blossom then
 or now

It doesn't matter

The flower doesn't know or care it has a name

It only knows the sun beckons it forth on this April day

Phillip is gone

and the no longer child
who once conquered this bank in two great leaps

Sits in a filtered sun
and wonders at the lavender star's newness
and that the lace of life, the bullheads, and leeches
that once were
are still
and will be
for other children to recall in spring

Concrete Poetry

One of the most enjoyable assignments that came out of *Words in the Blood* was the Concrete Poetry Assignment based on "Round Dance: An Iroquois Song" by Brian Swann. This assignment allowed student poets to achieve a level of artistry and creativity which was fun as well as sensitive and insightful. Concrete poetry should be interpreted as a visual as well as literary art. In creating concrete poetry, students are asked to use the space on the white page, the shape of the letter, and the words, the rhythm of the language to create a poem which *looks* like its subject. In other words, a concrete poem which works has letters, words and phrases which are placed on the white space of the page to look like or suggest in some visual way the subject of the poem. So that a concrete poem about a snake is shaped like a snake and tells something about the snake. A concrete poem about a drum is shaped like a drum and sounds like a drum when read aloud. A poem depicting a dance dances on the page. These poems are a challenge, but an enjoyable one, as students put all of their creative talents to work in developing a poem which is also a work of visual art (see Chapter 8 for student exemplars).

Art Activities for the Native American Cultural Study

Literature Base: *Words In The Blood: Contemporary Indian Writers of North and South America*, by Jamake Highwater

This Ethnic Week program was probably the students' favorite cultural study because they live within the same environment and have personally related to the Native American within their everyday existence. With each educational activity, an educator hopes to find a windfall. We were most fortunate to have a windfall with this cultural unit. The movie *Dances With Wolves* made its debut two months prior to our designated unit. By the time we introduced this unit of study, almost every student had viewed this movie and had already developed a concern and interest in the Native American Indians. Our hope in doing this study was to provide the students with the gift of knowledge concerning the spirit of these people that developed long ago and which still exists today. We wanted to eliminate stereotypes and common place misunderstandings which inhibit learning.

The art activities that developed during this unit involved students from all four art teachers in our department. These teachers, Royce Fleming, Mike Callaway, Cindy Daniels, and myself, became instrumental in providing units of study in the areas of pottery, painting, and drawing. Specific assignments were developed by each teacher for their individual classes and teaching styles. All of the work developed during this unit was placed on display in the library during Ethnic Week.

The literature base for this study was *Words In The Blood* by Jamake Highwater. We used this specific book as the basis for our classes because we felt that it was rich in language, traditions and customs that captured the spirit of the Native American. This cultural study was the third involvement of this kind of activity for the art students and by this time they knew how to investigate and research the diversity of another culture. The students were asked to read any part or all of the book given to them in order to start to develop a sketchbook of symbols, images, customs, and beliefs concerning as many areas as possible about the Native American. The art staff collected additional resources on Native American art forms, symbols, and developed a visual dictionary for the students to use as they created their individual projects. The students were asked to draw features of the Native American and record ornamentations found within the Native American environment. The sketchbook could contain notes, drawings, Native American words, verbal phrases that were significant to the student from the translated passages in *Words In The Blood*. The length of each student's sketchbook varied tremendously. However, after spending two class periods working in their sketchbook all of the students had ample time to develop their individual feelings toward the Native American spirit.

Upon the completion of their sketchbooks, students spent time in small groups looking over each other's sketchbook information. The students were also allowed time to share their favorite passages from our selected reading, *Words In The Blood*. The students liked best the selected reading, *Blue Highways*, by William Least Heat Moon. In this work, the writer discusses the *Book of Hopi*, which addresses the Hopi belief that human existence is essentially a series of journeys and a pattern that every human being moves within. This story included a visualization or picture of their journey and I could see the students making personal comparisons of their beliefs with these Hopi beliefs as well as gain a greater appreciation for the complexity of these people.

The art staff displayed works of art created by George Catlin and Albert Bierstadt, as these early American artists provided an impact to our history by recording the Native American. Contemporary Native American Artists were also studied in video form. We provided the students with three hours of a PBS Video Series entitled *The American Indian Artists.* These videos were personal interviews with Medicine Flower, Lone Wolf, Allan Houser, Fritz Scholder, Charles Loloma, and Helen Hardin. These artists came alive to us as they discussed their heritage, art, and their responsibilities to preserve their culture through the arts.

Most of the student assignments for this cultural project were based on the spiritual symbolism of the culture. Because so much of the Native American world is sacred and spiritual, the students were to develop imagery that would convey their understanding of the Native American.

Students in commercial design were asked to develop black-and-white sacred circles. The use of a circle was selected as it is significant to the Native American culture. These circles could have been developed using existing or known Native American symbols from their sketchbooks or they could "reinvent the wheel" and develop their own ideas that expressed their new understanding of this culture. These circles were to be a final visualization created from their writings and ideas developed in their sketchbooks. The students finished projects, their sacred circles, were completed in pen and ink and placed on 18" x 18" paper. Upon completion, these projects were laminated and matted for display purposes.

The drawing students worked in mixed media and were to develop a visual image that told of the heritage of the Native American. Because of the Native Americans' strong respect for animals and their rich spiritual relationship to their environment, much of the student work developed around this relationship. They worked in mixed medias on 18" x 24" paper. Upon completing their work, they matted it for display.

The painting class used tempera and developed images from their sketchbooks. These students were asked to depict one day in the life of a Native American. Many students required additional resources to further develop their ideas and the librarians were instrumental in fostering their individual needs. Children's books were most helpful in giving all of us a broader understanding of one day in the life of the Native American.

The ceramic students studied Native American pottery, viewed videos pertaining to this subject and developed hand built ceramic pieces that were embellished with variations of Native American designs.

When the students completed their art work, they were asked to write a poem that explained their work. The writings were completed from their sketchbook ideas, as well as from their finished work. This assignment was not graded but served to communicate the students visual message in one additional manner. Many of the students used the book *Words in the Blood* also to refresh their minds and to enhance their writings. Their written assignments were assembled together and placed into a book format for sharing. Each student received a copy and we spent time reading their work together.

Our grading of student work always pertains to specific objectives that they are provided with at the beginning of each unit of study. Students are graded on their understanding of media used, techniques which have been demonstrated in class and which are to be mastered and in their crafts-manship. We also evaluate the students' creativity, sense of purpose or expression—that refers to the subject matter selected and their under-standing of this topic. Student self-evaluations, both oral and written, are important in developing a visual vocabulary, and also contribute signifi-cantly in establishing goals for self-improvement in the arts. All of these projects took approximately three weeks to complete and the finished work positively reflected their new appreciation for Native Americans.

All of our classes participated in the library forums and benefited by actually hearing speakers, seeing dancers and listening to the spirit of another culture.

Chapter 8
Discovering the Path to a New Past
and Present

Robyn Butterfield, Pen and Ink

Jason Taliaferro, Mixed Media

Indian
by Jerad Widman
(Found Poem. Character. *Words in the Blood***)**
Instructor: Doug Goheen

1.
He hated them
Not for what they wanted
to do with him
but for what they did to the earth
With their machines
and to the animals
with their packs of dogs and their guns
It happened again
and again
And the people had to watch
Unable to save
or to protect
any of the things
that were so important to them

2.
He took careful aim
pulling the bowstring taut
But just a second before he shot
the string broke

3.
And gently
        like the stroke of soft feathered birds
the eyes of the man of thunder and lightning
        fell upon the people
        His touched them
and they moved quietly
        like dying angels
                floating like memories
                        to the arm

A Little of My Blood
by Jennifer Orr
(Found Poem. *Words in the Blood*)

A little of my blood
Runs deep into my flesh
The lines of my arteries
Travel along the dust of my ancèstry
When the trails narrow into dust
You are no longer my blood.

Yellow and Black Colors
by Tim Fisher
(Nature Poetry Assignment)

The yellow and black colors
Streak across the blue
Sky
With bright white
Clouds.
He swivels in and out of
Trees, looking for his goal.
With wings fluttering
He sees his
Target.
Unmercifully
He dives
Down, going against
The wind. With his
Heart
Pumping
He
Reaches out for the
One thing he
Strives
For.
Finally he reaches for what he
Could have
Lost:

His life
The pollen
Of a flower.

Grasshopper
by Tim Bruce
(Found Poem. *Words in the Blood*)

Sleeping by the lake
Often I do
I woke to find
Not of my blood
But that of a grasshopper

Thoughts fell into dreams
As they may of storms
For in six days was
The coming of winter
By tomorrow he won't be

Hesitant and fearful
The foolishness of him
Had passed away

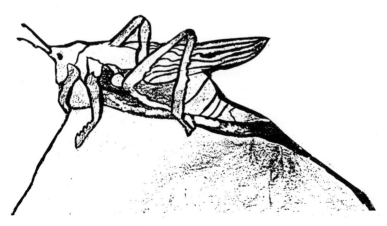

Tim Bruce, Mixed Media

Waxy Cactus Flowers
by Alex Burtin
(Found Poem. *Words in the Blood)*

As pure and clear as ice
man soaked up the sun's warmth
with chicalote blossoms
and white poppies

Alex Burtin, Mixed Media

Warm Earth Beneath My Feet
by Wendy Whiteside
(Chant Poem. *Words in the Blood)*

Customs buried beside my ancestors
Warm Earth Beneath My feet

Who once felt this same
Warm Earth Beneath Their Feet
Tanned toes slowly sift
Warm Earth Beneath My Feet

Tender shoots of new grass
Warm Earth Beneath My Feet

Brown is the Blood
Warm Earth Beneath My Feet

Green is the Life
Warm Earth Beneath My Feet

Jennifer Long
Concrete Poem inspired by
Words in the Blood

```
        heritage.      in  my
          lost            euphoria
        forget          This living
       to never         child inside
       prairie,            of me.
        native           My hope
      eternity on        My dream has
       Spending         come true.
      and esteem        The chiefs do
       high glory       Their  dance
      shall be of       And sing
       His name         their praises
         honor.     in  this  precious
          child's
```

Inner Sanctuary
by Tricia Quinn
(Found Poem. *Words in the Blood*)

Gazing into my inner sanctuary
Like an eye looking into the sky
Confusion fills the air
Giving me a light sense of insecurity
His shadow peers at me
With his look
My blood halts
His own heart and flesh is cold
Giving me the knowledge it has ended.

My Spirit Comes Here to Drink
by Brent Venis
(Found Poem. *Words in the Blood*)

I am of this coast and its keeper
And my spirit comes here to drink
Surrounded by spirits of caring
As a timber blue haze dissolves
The mountains snow covered and glowing
Wolf will soon drop winter fur
This afternoon it will rain
Bringing beauty of grain
My spirit comes here to drink.

Lynette Grandstaff, Tempera Painting

Stacey Nodolf, Pen and Ink

Concrete Poems inspired by *Words in the Blood*

```
                    DANCING AROUND
        THEIR NEWBORN BEAUTY    NEW DUSK
         THE ONCE DEAD BRANCHES    NEW MORN
          HELP PEOPLE IN NEED       THE DAY WHISPERS
          TO SLAY THE EVILS         ANIMALS SCURRY
        OF WINTER HEARTS               TO WAKE US ALL
      A DAY OF NEW BEGINNINGS       THE SUN COMES
          AND JUST BORN             FROM ITS SLUMBER
           THE DAY IS NEW          WAKING THE NEW CHILD
           THE STARS GO AWAY       THE PETALS OF A FLOWER
           THE MOON FADES          OPEN TO SEE THE DAY
                    WE  DANCE, DANCE

                           -MEGAN BOTSFORD
```

SNAKE

By
slides
and slithers
the snake
sneaks
to
catch his
prey. Back
and forth
he winds
and writhes
nothing can
escape. Hypnotized
by ruinous rhythm
the snake brings
certain death.
Movements of
defense cause
coils to fold.
Foiling all
breaks
from
the
will
of a
snake

Eleanor Turner

Christie Schafer, Pen and Ink

The Scream of the Hawk
by Greg Thayer

The sky was gray and overcast. Mist had covered the concrete of the parking lot and the assorted cars with a light dew. It appeared that the colors had been leached out of everything, leaving them pale and lifeless. Cooper looked out at the dreary landscape, the view from his dorm room reflecting what he felt inside. He broke his attention away from the scene and turned back to his text. Finals were coming up, for which he was vaguely grateful. It gave him something to do, an excuse to study, an excuse to turn down the invitations to parties he didn't want to go to. He always felt awkward, unwanted at such social gatherings, as if the others hadn't really wanted him there but had asked out of politeness.

He received good grades, but he didn't assign them much value. He worked for them because it was expected of him, because he didn't want to make waves or disappoint anyone. He realized that he spent most of his time attempting to be anonymous, unnoticed, invisible. In spite of that, he always stood out in a crowd.

With a disgusted snort, he slammed his book shut and bounced up from the bed. It was useless to try to study when his thoughts kept wandering like scared sparrows. He stalked into the bathroom, turned on the water, and splashed his face with it. His mind cleared at the rush of cold. He raised his head and looked into the mirror over the sink. His long, straight, black hair framed his face. His high cheekbones, dark eyes, and brown skin gave evidence of his heritage. Yet most people commented that he resembled his father most.

His self-examination was interrupted when the phone rang. He picked up the phone, surprise registering on his face when he heard his mother's voice.

He remembered listening to his father, saying that sometimes you just had to drop everything and start over. The present circumstances showed that phrase in a new light. He turned it over in his mind, then realized that it applied to him to. He grinned, confident now that a plan of action had presented itself.

The scream of the hawk broke the stillness of the early morning desert. Cooper awoke from his fitful sleep. His thin sleeping bag hadn't cushioned the bumpy ground, and his back was sore. In an attempt to ward off the threatening stiffness, he dressed quickly, gathered up his gear into his backpack, and set off towards the dawning sun.

As Cooper walked, he noticed the diverse wildlife of the desert wake around him. Small lizards scuttled out of dark nooks and crannies onto sunny rocks to warm their cold blood. Kangaroo rats and jack rabbits watched curiously as Cooper approached, then fled when he came closer. Desert marigold and brittlebush flowers added to the natural beauty. In the distance he could see the outline of a hawk against the sky. Again he heard its lonely cry.

After an hour of walking though the shifting sand and rock outcroppings, he settled into the shade of a mesquite tree and ate from his supply of dried fruits, beef jerky, and similar traveler's delicacies. He ran his hand through his straight hair, feeling the exquisite workmanship of the silver and turquoise hair clip he wore. It had been made by his mother, who was full blooded Navajo. Cooper removed it, looked thoughtfully at it, then gently hung it on a branch. He also removed his watch, which had been made by his father and was of similar silver and turquoise design, and placed it on the same branch. It seemed right to him that he should go on without them while he was in the desert. After several swallows from his canteen, Cooper was on his way again, unfettered and unmarked by his past. His long black hair swung at the back of his neck, and his bare wrist was lighter than the rest of his arm. The tree was soon left far behind.

It was the hottest time of the desert. Most wildlife had taken refuge from the blazing heat. Seeking sanctuary, Cooper had to settle for the indifferent protection of a high reaching mesa. But it blocked out little of the sun, which was almost directly overhead. He walked around the solitary tower, looking for a crevice or cave in which he could find shelter.

As he walked around the finger of rock, he found no cave, but he noticed that there was a ridge, almost a path, that rose up to the top of the mesa. At one point it was shaded by an overhang. Cooper rested there, leaning back against the relatively cool rock, looking up at the indigo sky. He saw the shape of a hawk, black against the sky, circle and come to a rest at the top of the mesa. Its shrill cry echoed the loneliness in Cooper's soul, making him shudder despite the heat.

He looked at his wrist, then remembered that he had left his watch behind. Then he realized that here, the time or even the date had no meaning. He almost regretted leaving it, and his hair clip. They had been his most valued possessions. But he wanted no reminders of his parents right now. For several years their's had been a happy marriage, but lately it had become strained. They had recently told him that they were getting a divorce. He hadn't been surprised, but that didn't make it any easier.

The worst of the heat had passed, and life returned to the world. Cooper rose from his light nap and considered his prospects. Instead of hiking on, he decided to climb to the mesa and camp on its summit.

Like most mesas, it was a tall, thin tower of rock. The harder stone at the top protected the stone below it from erosion, while the soft stone around it was worn away by wind and water. The slope was almost vertical, but the handy ledge would give him excellent leverage, braced against the sides.

The climb was as easy as he had predicted—at first. But as the slope steepened he had to take more time. The cleft became shallower, and he had to carefully plan each handhold, testing each to be sure it would hold his weight. But when he reached the overhang that had previously protected him from the sun the danger of falling was so great he was tempted to go back. Even if he made it to the top, getting down would be another story. But he forged ahead, ignoring the risks, knowing that the more he thought about what he was doing, the more real the danger became. At one point he had to rely on his hands alone, as there was no purchase for his feet on the more than vertical slope below. Alarmingly, the tiny ledge his left hand clung to was slowly crumbling under his weight. Cursing, Cooper searched for a more secure hold, but the only one he saw was out of reach for his left hand. Desperately, he swung from side to side, gaining momentum, as his grip disintegrated. Finally he lunged for his new perch with his right hand, praying it would be better than his last.

The stress on the ledge was too much, and it gave way totally, almost before his right hand grasped its own ledge. Quickly he found one hold after another, scrambling up the slope too fast to test a position's strength, until once again he could rest his weight on his feet.

With less than a fourth of the way to go, he paused to regain his breath. He heard flapping sounds from above. Startled, he looked at the top, which was surprisingly close. Small pebbles fell from above. Something was up there. He watched intently, but nothing showed. Curious, he started climbing again, dragging his fatigue like a leaden weight.

He was only a few handholds from the top when a midnight black shape flew out from above, shrieking and scratching. He felt the hawk's claws tear at his hands, leaving tracks that burned with cold. Forgetting his precarious position, he waved his arms in an attempt to scare the bird off. He began to slide, and threw himself against the cliff wall. His entire body pressed against the mesa, his fall had stopped but he had no defense against the mysterious avian attacker. Again and again, it raked its claws against his back, leaving freezing cuts, and flapped its wings against his head, trying to dislodge him. But he held on, knowing that release was death. Balked, the bird broke off its attack and winged away, its scream echoing off the mesa.

Cooper rested at the summit, nursing his wounds. Night had fallen long ago, and he had taken some dead branches from the single tree which grew on the lonely pinnacle. He had placed the branches in a circle and lit them to ward off the cold. It was now well past midnight, but he felt no need for sleep.

He reflected on what had happened. His wounds were not deep, but the chill he felt from them worried him. And the strangest thing was that he had scratches on his back and arms, where they had been protected by his shirt and even back pack, but his clothes were unmarked. Only his flesh had been affected.

He wondered about the nature of the bird itself. He had seen it clearly when it had flown down at him. It had been a deep, impenetrable black. He couldn't kid himself that it was merely the contrast between the dark hawk and the bright sky. It had been black, and that was all it had been. It was as if a hole had been cut out in the rough shape of a raptor, then animated. Its wings had been devoid of feathers, its head featureless. It had been nothing but a silhouette.

He remembered his mother, Nadine, telling him tales of supernatural creatures when he was young. His father, Mark, had also given him a rich history of the unearthly. His stories had been classic myths, but hers had been original stories. She told them as if they had actually happened to her. Many were the nights when Cooper had listened entranced to his mother spinning tales of magic. As a child, he had not understood, and had thought of the stories as fairy tales. But now, at eighteen, he felt that some of what his mother had told him must have held some truth.

His father had lived most of his life out in the sun. The rest of the time he was designing and making jewelry. In his youth, Mark had often gone into the same desert Cooper now visited. He had met Nadine while she was also hiking across the desert. She had been bored with life on the reservation, and young enough to still be rebellious. They were married not long after. They lived in L.A. for many years—running a jewelry store. But later, Nadine had wanted to return to her family. Mark was willing, and they moved out to the reservation. But they often returned to the city to oversee the shop.

Cooper spent his life shuttling between two extremes. He schooled at the reservation and L.A., but he didn't feel like he fit in at either place. He was Indian, yet he didn't know all of what that meant or could mean. His parents were his refuge; they knew him and he was connected to the world through them. And if they no longer existed as a family, what was his place? When he found that his parents were divorcing, he pulled out of college. He remembered that his father had often gone to the desert when he was troubled. Cooper hoped he could do the same.

He shuddered and looked away from the fire. Actually, the night was not too cold. Some of the day's heat had not yet escaped into the cloudless sky. But Cooper's chill was deeper. He stood and walked to the edge, and looked out over the nightscape. There was no moon, and the stars provided little illumination. The fire showed the small area atop the mesa and little else. Directly below was darkness. It was as if he was suspended over a bottomless abyss on a tiny shard of land.

He looked up at the sky. Without light pollution from the city, the stars shone clearly and bright. He picked out the constellations of the Zodiac. As he watched, he saw several stars blink once. Cooper felt a chill of apprehension. His fears were confirmed when he heard its scream. Anxiously, he took a step forward, scanning the sky. He stopped just short of the precipitous edge. The number of stars eclipsed by the approaching bird grew larger. Cooper's breath caught as he anticipated another attack. But this time he was not trapped against a high stone wall. He was on top of a high mesa, on the edge of a small overhang. An overhang which consisted of only a foot of weak stone, which slowly crumbled while Cooper's attention was distracted; a foot of weak stone which suddenly broke away from under him.

His stomach jumped into his throat as the world flew apart around him. He fell into the darkness, the lone source of light speeding away from him. Wind blew past him, whistling through his ears.

Suddenly he felt a wrenching, momentary pain in his back as he struck an outcropping of the mesa. He spun away, away from the mesa, away from the light. He saw the edge of a half-circle of firelight above him. A portion was suddenly blanked out by the hawk.

He spun until the mesa top was out of sight. Below him there was only darkness. Even the faint starlight illuminated nothing. The fierce wind rushed past him at rising speeds, sucking the warmth from his body.

He was facing up again. Now he couldn't see any stars, and the thin crescent of light had turned into a perfect circle. The edges of the circle periodically flashed as the hawk's wings covered them. He looked below, trying to see how far away the ground was. His blind terror turned to amazement that he hadn't hit yet. But below him was nothing. And he felt that even had there been light there would have been nothing to see. He was freezing.

The circle of light was no longer an outline, and he could clearly see the hawk. Its outline seemed rougher, less clear cut, more real. He even thought he could see its feathers. It tucked in its wings and dove towards him. Idly, he wondered if it would reach him before he hit the ground. He knew he should be panicking, but he felt strangely calm. He was so cold he didn't feel or hear the wind anymore, and his extremities were numb.

The hawk was very near to him. Almost all of its features were real now, except its head. Behind it the circle of light looked like a tunnel, leading back to the desert sky. It appeared to be early dawn, up there.

Below him was the eternal blackness, and the mind-numbing cold. There was no land here, he realized. If there had been any, even allowing for distortions of his temporal sense, he would have hit it long ago. All feeling was gone, and he was free of emotions. He felt empty, as if he wasn't really there, as if he was only an outline, a construction, a remnant of what he used to be. His only sense was sight.

The tunnel was now clearly defined. It seemed to reach up forever, to that tiny circle of light and life and warmth. The hawk was almost to him now, and he could see its feathers blowing in a wind he could not feel. Its head was now visible, except for the eyes, which remained cold and lifeless.

The utter, complete darkness was now broken by something else. Cooper dimly saw the outline of a monstrous, hideous figure. It was visible only as a darker shade of the abyss. It reached for him hungrily. Cooper now felt fear, more fear than he had felt when he had first fell, before he hit the rock and had that pain in this back.

"Omygod," he thought, amazed, "I'm dead."

He felt the hawk's claws sink in, into, through his back, the wings overlay arms he could no longer sense. Surprisingly, the hawk was warm like the sun, warm like the real world.

The beast below reached for him with tones of black and cold, its invisible mouth opened in a roar of anger as it saw its prey escape.

Cooper flexed his wings and flew up through the tunnel.

A hawk could dimly be seen, perched in the shadows, on the mesa. It sat unmoving, watching a shifting figure lying on the sands below it. The figure's back was bent at an odd angle, but still it moved, not knowing it was dead. Gradually it slowed its tortured movements. As the sun rose, the shadow moved to cast more light upon it. The diffuse light showed wings, claws, but all else was still in darkness. The shadow moved, covering the young man, who had almost stopped moving altogether. Only his face was still in the sun, his features calming, then twisting in a grimace of fear. Suddenly a look of surprise covered the man's face, the lips moving as if speaking, then he relaxed, at peace. Dead.

The mesa's shadow moved, obscuring the entire body. The hawk came into the light. It shook itself, then launched into the air. It flew high and strong, the dawning sun gleaming off its bright, intelligent eyes. Behind it left only the unwanted reminders of the past: a dim column of smoke from a burned-out fire on top of the mesa, some camping gear next to the embers, and the outline of a body in the sand at the mesa's base.

And the only sound was the scream of the hawk.

Shawn Miller, Tempera Painting

Chapter 9

The Path Leads to America
The Hmong

Emily Eakes, Linoleum Print

Yee Chang and Chu Vue

The library was overcrowded, filled with noisy students waiting once again to hear speakers for an Ethnic Week forum. The difference this time was that the speakers were two apparently average Asian-American men not too much older than the students themselves. With some difficulty, the room was quieted and David Moore, a retired high school teacher spoke of how he had gained a family from his involvement as a scout leader with young Hmong students who had arrived in the late 1970's to his school in Minneapolis. He then introduced Chu Vue, his "adopted son," and Yee Chang another member of Boy Scout Troop 100 to the audience of teenagers.

Chu was an unassuming figure. He wore old-fashioned spectacles, a wide smile, and spoke with a remarkably slight accent. He cheerfully told of his journey to America; only frowning once as he recalled how he had arrived without his immediate family. They had been killed. He spoke then of his gratitude to America and how, though he would always long for the mountains of Laos, he felt this would always be his home. He told how his father and other Hmong men had been recruited by the CIA to fight for America in the war. There was no boast in his voice: no complaint about the great sacrifice his family had made; no hint of self-pity. Chu was proud that his family had chosen freedom over communist rule. He was positive about his future and explained that he was currently in the midst of a university career. He also told the students that had he led the life of his parents he would have been married at the age of fifteen and he would already have several children. He told of how it was to come to America from a tropical climate in the midst of a Minnesota January—barefoot and unfamiliar with even the technology of a flush toilet. He told of a kind African-American woman who, upon seeing him playing in the snow without any shoes, had brought some to him. The students' empathy was tangible. Chu was a lesson in courage.

If Chu was a lesson in courage, his companion, Yee Chang, was a lesson in optimism. The students were captivated by Yee on sight. He stood before them dressed in a brilliant red shirt shimmering with row upon row of tiny silver medals that softly chimed with every movement Yee made. He told the students the story of his family coming to America and he laughed at himself for not knowing how to work a doorknob. He spoke of the love the Hmong had for nature and how he and the other Hmong scouts loved the wilderness. He told of how beautiful their mountain home in

Laos had been and how they missed the warm climate. He also showed the students a large wooden top which he explained no Hmong child in Laos would be without. He then threw the top and it spun magnificently. Yee told us all of this with a beautiful, winning smile. yet there was a hint of melancholy in his voice as he explained that the Hmong culture, the culture of the heritage so dear to him had with so many Hmong men, women, and children apparently also become a casualty of the war. In coming to America, to survive the Hmong had been forced to assimilate at an extraordinary pace. Yee and Chu explained that already (in the short span of just fifteen years) there were Hmong children who had no idea of their culture, their language, their history—in short no idea who they were.

The students were visibly moved by Chu's quiet acceptance of his fate, and Yee's warmth and playfulness as well as both young men's deep appreciation of what America had to offer. They had captured our students imaginations and hearts. And they each had helped them to look at their country as something beautiful, rare, and wonderful. A place that strangers worlds away had died for.

Language Arts Activities for a Study of Asian Americans

Literature Base: *World Mythology: An Anthology of the Great Myths and Epics*, edited by Donna Rosenberg

World Mythology is an anthology of the best known myths from throughout the world. It is specifically intended to be used as a text book for the study of mythology as a literature course for grades nine through twelve. It is inevitable that Ethnic Week activities lend themselves to a course in mythology. Mythology is, after all, the study of the stories which depict the beliefs of various peoples and their cultures. This book includes myths of China. Since the major focus of Ethnic Week 1992 would be the Hmong culture, students studied Chinese mythology concurrently with Ethnic Week because the Hmong had fled from Northern China as refugees to the mountains of Laos. What they focused upon were the creation myths of China and the myths' explanation of the Chinese as a "chosen people." Students gained insight into how myths may affect the way in which people treat one another and how creation myths often lead to a belief in the exclusion of others outside of a given culture. The Chinese myths read from *World Mythology* included "The Creation of the Universe and Human Beings," and "Yi the Archer and the Ten Suns."

Prior to reading these myths, students were given a short lecture (fifteen minutes) on the relationship of China to the Hmong. They were told that the Hmong had first made their homes in China, although they were not Chinese. It was at this point in time, that students discussed the importance of myths, folk tales and legends in separating one culture from another. We discussed how the myths they were studying were uniquely Chinese.

Within the myth "The Creation of the Universe and Human Beings" the Chinese creator, Pangu is depicted as intelligent, industrious, and unselfish. He represents the best of Chinese males. He decides what he wants to do and accomplishes it with infinite patience, determination, and perseverance. Nugua is the female mother goddess within this myth. She has a creative intelligence. She surveys nature with a mind that notices details, both great and small, and she can imagine what it lacks and how to create it. As she creates, she becomes easily bored with what she is doing, so she tries different methods. She accepts the fact that her two processes create different products. However, the human beings formed from her first creative endeavor and who possess the greatest intelligence and wealth are, of course, Chinese.

The myth "Yi the Archer and the Ten Suns" depicts a hero, Yi, who is both divine and human. In this myth, the world originally had ten suns who misbehave and disrupt the order of the universe just for the fun of it. They get tired of traveling across the heavens as they are supposed to do and instead of traveling one by one they decide to travel together all ten at once. As a result, they create great havoc, and it is left to Yi to destroy all but one of the suns and thus bring order to the universe. Thus evil is depicted as a chance occurrence rather than a premeditated one. The gods are not vengeful, and correct behavior on the part of human beings will not assure the absence of evil. The lesson here is that people must accept whatever comes because they cannot hope to avoid or change it.

Procedures and Activities

The Biopoem and the Telling of an Original Myth

Following the reading of these two myths, students were required to write a Biopoem (see Chapter 3 for a detailed description of this assignment) in which they wrote about one of the major characters within the myths. Students were then asked to develop their own stories in which they took the characters of these stories (Yi, Pangu, and Nugua) and created their own myths. The requirement was that they stay true to the character of these Chinese deities and try to create a myth which captured the character of these deities. After they completed their writing, students then shared their original myth with the class. Since the original stories of Pangu, Nugua and Yi were from an oral tradition, students were not required to turn in a written story, but rather were required to share their myths orally with the class. The teacher modeled this assignment with her own myth on the same day she handed the assignment to the class. The assignment follows:

> You are to develop your own Chinese creation myth using one or all of these characters from Chinese mythology: Pangu, Nugua, or Yi the Archer. Your creation myth will not be turned in as a written assignment, but rather will be told aloud to your fellow students and teacher. The classroom will become an ancient Chinese village, and you will be the Village Elder or Storyteller. The requirement will be that your myth provide a moral, explain something which occurs in nature, or uses Yi the Archer as a hero in a situation in which he teaches us how to be brave. You may work with a partner in developing this myth and you will be allowed three class periods to perfect your story. Your myth should take at least seven minutes to tell and should be no longer than fifteen minutes. If you like, you may also wear a costume or bring props, but remember to stay in the character of an ancient storyteller.

Students had fun completing this assignment, and it lead nicely into Ethnic Week, as students came to a clearer understanding of an oral tradition, through the development of their own myths. As a result, students became sensitive to the importance of the storyteller in the Hmong tradition as they listened and learned about the story cloths and the journey the Hmong had made to Laos from China and then to the United States.

Literature Base: *Dark Sky, Dark Land: Stories of the Hmong Boy Scouts of Troop 100*, by David L. Moore.

Dark Sky, Dark Land: Stories of the Hmong Boy Scouts of Troop 100 is a book written by the Boy Scout troop leader of a group of young men who were Hmong refugees to the United States in the 1970s. The individual stories of these remarkably brave and heroic young men may be easily read by students from the seventh through twelfth grades. In telling the stories of the Scouts in his troop, Mr. Moore simply states the facts of what happened to these young men. It is up to the reader to discern what is not stated: the stark terror of war, the desolation of a refugee camp, the utter loneliness which must have been felt by these young people as they came from a mountain home where even a simple doorknob is unheard of and into the technologically advanced United States.

This book became a catalyst for finding out more about the Hmong and the plight of refugees everywhere through providing a basis for researching the events surrounding the Hmong's loss of home, the war in Southeast Asia, and the haven which the United States can be. Because of our involvement in previous Ethnic Week activities involving Apartheid, the Holocaust, and the Native American, students were sensitive to those who were culturally and unjustly disenfranchised. This was to their credit and benefit in approaching a study of the Hmong. The Hmong had a history of using folk art in the form of story cloths or stitchery to tell their stories, as well as a strong oral tradition. Study of the Hmong provided students not only with new insights into an unknown culture of recent American immigrants, but also provided a deeper understanding of oral folk literature and in the process challenged their written voices.

Procedures and Activities

The Killing Fields

The feature film *The Killing Fields* was used to bring stories represented in *Dark Sky, Dark Land* to life in the following ways. It told the story of the devastation of the war in Southeast Asia from the perspective of a disenfranchised Cambodian (who shared a great deal in common with the Hmong). It personalized the tragedy of war. It spoke to the morality of leaving an ally behind. Although this film has an "R" rating, some profane language, and depicts the graphic violence of war, it is a powerful message about what family, home, friendship, and faith meant in the utter desolation of the war in Southeast Asia. The film makes clear the trauma of that war from the perspective of a refugee better than any other resource. Because of this, students' parents were asked for permission to show the film. And it was viewed prior to their being given the book *Dark Sky, Dark Land*. Students were moved by the film. It succeeded in creating just what

the text of *Dark Sky, Dark Land* needed: images which conveyed the
horror and courage of surviving a war and looking to the United States for
refuge.

Before viewing the film, one class period was spent discussing the war
with the focus being the Hmong involvement as our allies fighting for the
CIA. *Dark Sky, Dark Land* provides some very good information about
the history of the Hmong as a group of people who have a long past of
disenfranchisement with survival. Three points were emphasized during
this class period.

1. The Hmong had been our staunchest allies in the War in Southeast
   Asia.
2. The Hmong were struggling for identity in the United States.
3. One of their greatest tragedies was that their children reared in the
   United States may not understand or know their own culture.

Immediately after viewing the film (which took two full fifty-minute
class periods), students wrote their visual impression of the film. Students
were allowed exactly ten minutes to complete this writing. This was
followed by a writing in which students wrote for five minutes defining
war, and for five minutes defining peace. We then broke into small groups
(no larger than five) to share our observations. As a class, we spent ten
minutes discussing what a hero was and whether or not they thought they
could be heroic in the midst of such utter devastation. Students then wrote
for twenty minutes about how they thought it would feel to flee their
homes in order to save their own and their families' lives, only to find
themselves in a land that is not only foreign in the sense that it has a
language barrier—but is geographically, climatically, culturally, and technologically a new world. We spent two class periods discussing this film
and these writings. Students were passionate in their sympathy for the
Cambodians depicted in the film, and enthusiastic about the possibility of
learning more about such refugees.

Creating a Voice for the Hmong

Drama is very difficult to write. Using staging and dialogue only, the
writer must convey all the human emotion, trauma, triumph and tragedy
needed to engage an audience. One thing which is striking about the
stories in *Dark Sky, Dark Land* is that they are dramatic. Yet they are not
drama, and do not engage an audience. Prior to their involvement in this

unit of study, none of the students had ever heard of the Hmong. yet by the end of the first week of study, students felt that the Hmong deserved to be understood, nurtured within our society, and preserved as a culture. The first assignment students completed was to find a voice for the Hmong through reading one of the selections in the book and creating a monologue for a person whose story is being told. This provided sophomore English students with a deeper understanding of how nonfiction can lead to characterization and voice in the creation of fiction or docudrama (such as the screen play for *The Killing Fields*). Students were allowed to work in pairs as they developed these monologues, or, if they wished, work alone. Two class periods were spent working on their monologues and two class periods were spent presenting the monologues to the class in short skits. However, prior to completing the "polished" skits the class attended library forums in which they met David Moore, the author of *Dark Sky, Dark Land* and two of the young men whose stories had been told in the book. Of course, this added a depth to the students' work which otherwise would have been lacking. And in providing faces to the heroes depicted in Moore's story of the Hmong, it also added a depth to their understanding and empathy for human suffering which will remain with these students throughout their lives.

Writing a Play

The Drama of the Hmong Story

Dark Sky, Dark Land and the study of the Hmong during Ethnic week became a starting point for the teaching of dramatic writing. One sophomore student, Peter Wedel, was particularly successful in his attempt at dramatizing the story of the Hmong through a play in which he depicts the escape to Thailand and eventual life in America for one Hmong refugee. Peter's play (see Chapter 10 for Peter Wedel's play, *Pan Dow*) shows great pathos and it is worth depicting here how he went through the process of developing it.

Peter's research began with the reading of Moore's book. Following this, he realized that he needed to do a great deal more research in order to develop the story which would later be worked into dialog and finally a play. Peter went to Mike Printz, our librarian, for help in continuing his research. Peter was allowed to take home our class packet of information which had been provided by the library for the study of the Hmong. Mr. Printz provided Peter with still more magazine articles and he showed

Peter how to use the DIALOG computer search to gain more current or obscure information about the Hmong. Peter said that this search helped him to feel more secure about the accuracy of what he was writing. Students are always allowed access to our school's writing center and Peter did most of his composing at a computer in the writing center. His first step, however was taking notes on what he read as he did his research. Our school has an extensive collection of *National Geographic* magazines dating from the 1920s, and some of the most helpful information was provided by issues dating from the 1960s which provided colorful photographs of the Hmong in their mountain homes in Laos prior to the displacement created by the war. These helped Peter to see how he would set the stage for his characters as his play developed.

Peter worked in writing workshops which consisted of a group of four students to "talk through" what he would be doing with his writing. The play thus developed through this process.

1. Reading the stories in *Dark Sky, Dark Land.*
2. Continued library research.
3. Studying other biogrpahical plays. (The play *The Miracle Worker* about Helen Keller's relationship with Annie Sullivan is a good model for students attempting to write this type of drama.)
4. Sharing of his work in writing workshops with four other writing students.
5. Dialog between Peter and his teacher.

Peter was allowed a full month to complete his work. In the middle of this month, "Ethnic Week, Asian American Cultures" was scheduled to take place. During this week, David Moore, Yee Chang, and Chu Vue were scheduled to come and speak to Topeka West High School students. They would be spending two nights in Topeka, and they each needed a place to stay. Mike Printz knew that Peter was very serious about completing a play which depicted the story of the Hmong, and he suggested that one of our guests, Chu Vue, stay at Peter's house. Peter and his family were happy to welcome Chu into their home, and Peter and Chu became friends in the short span of time that Chu was with him. It was this more than anything else which inspired Peter to complete his work and give life to the Hmong story through his play.

It was at this point in the process of writing his play, that Peter developed his concept for the story the play would portray. While outlining doesn't always work as a tool for creative writing, Peter found it was

helpful to complete a type of outline in which he noted what his protagonist (modeled after Chu Vue) would go through within the context of
Peter's own creation. This also made it easier, after Peter had completed
writing the dialog, to go through and make the minor adjustments necessary to make the staging work. The entire process, from the concept of
writing a play, researching, going through Ethnic Week activities, writing
workshops, and completing a finished product, took Peter five weeks. The
finished play showcases the plight of the Hmong and Peter's deep understanding of this people, their culture and way of life. This play highlights
the Hmong heritage and the importance and beauty of their art. Through
all of his research, Peter came to an understanding of just how important
folk art, particularly their story cloths, is to the Hmong. And a story cloth
became the focal point for Peter's own tale of the Hmong's journey to an
American home.

Art Activities for the Hmong Cultural Studies

Literature Base: *Dark Sky Dark Land: Stories of the Hmong Boy
Scouts of Troop 100*, by David L. Moore

The art department's involvement with this Ethnic Week activities
concerning the Hmong culture was far more encompassing in student
population than our first project with the Apartheid study. Our first project
involved 125 students, however, the other three instructors in our art
department also took part in this project, making the student population
approximately 300 in number. Royce Fleming, Mike Callaway, and Steve
Elder deserve credit for being active educators with this project, and
served their students well in motivating strong visual imagery. Each
teacher was instrumental in presenting the necessary historical information on the Hmong culture, after which we all developed different assignments to broaden the visual base or presentation upon the completion of
this study. We developed our historical presentation from the following
four Hmong books given to us by our librarians.

Moore, David L. 1989. *Dark Sky, Dark Land: Stories of the Hmong
Boy Scouts of Troop 100*. Eden Prairie, MN: Tessera Publishing.

Chan, Anthony and Norma J. Livo. 1990. *Hmong Textile Designs.*
    MD: Stemmer House Publishers.
MacDowell, Marsha, 1988. *Hmong Folk Arts: A Guide for Teachers.*
    East Lansing, MI: Michigan State University Press.
MacDowell, Marsha, 1989. *Stories In Thread: Hmong Pictorial
    Embroidery.* East Lansing, MI: Michigan State University
    Press.

The Hmong culture did not have a written language until the 1950s,
therefore, the visual language established by the Hmong people was vast
and very interesting to our students. The Hmong have communicated their
traditions, beliefs, and customs through song, storytelling and with a
specific art form called "pa Ndau." The pa Ndau (pronounced pan downs)
are story cloths made of fine stitchery, embroidery, appliques, and in some
instances batik (a wax resist and dying process). The Hmong stitchery was
also incorporated into the Hmong traditional dress and decoration found
on everyday clothing items. These clothing items usually distinguished
subcultures within their culture, such as the White Hmong, Green Hmong
and others. For this study, we were fortunate in having on hand, from Mary
K. Chelton's private Hmong art collection, three actual pieces of Hmong
art work available for students to see. The students were impressed with
the intricacy of these works.

Michigan State University is a wonderful source to contact for additional Hmong information as it has a vast collection of Hmong textile art
in the University Art Museum. It also provides traveling exhibits of
Hmong pa Ndaus. Two of our primary art sources for this project were
created by the Michigan State University Art Museum.

To help the students develop an understanding of the symbolic Hmong
language, we provided a "design motif index" for each student to use. The
design motif index was invaluable for our study and was obtained from
the book *Hmong Folk Arts: A Guide for Teachers,* developed by Marsha
MacDowell, Folk Arts Curator at Michigan State University Museum. A
copy of this visual guide follows at the end of this chapter.

The first traditional pa Ndaus were usually geometric in design and
depicted a well understood symbolic visual language. Most of the earlier
story cloths were symmetrical and usually 18" x 18" in size. Many of the
early Hmong story cloths were created in hues of varied blues and blacks
and the subject matter usually depicted traditions and celebrations such
as births, marriages and deaths.

A second style of Hmong pa Ndaus depict myths, stories, beliefs, courtship games and Hmong's closeness to nature. These Hmong designs are usually 8 x 6 feet in size and very colorful. These story cloths depicted a time during which their culture was isolated from outside influences. This style of pa ndau is still being produced in Thailand resettlement camps today.

The third style of pa Ndaus or story cloths that we introduced to the student was created during and after the Hmong involvement with the United States and the Vietnam War. These story cloths depict their involvement, suffering and the changes that have occurred to them since 1950 to the present day. The colors often used in these Hmong story cloths usually have red, white, and blue as a dominant theme. While they continue to use symbolism, there is an increase in the use of the human figure and written language as a subtitle in their work.

These story cloths were used initially to communicate and celebrate their lives. However, today they are a major source of income for the people still living in the resettlement camps in Thailand.

At the end of this chapter, there are a few examples of the story cloths created by the Hmong which we shared with our students. These examples were selected because they represent historical change within the culture and all three styles of pa ndaus. These examples are reproduced from Anthony Chan's book, *Hmong Textile Designs.*

Procedures and Art Activities

After completing an overview of the Hmong and their vanishing way of life, students were asked to read one of the stories from David Moore's book, *Dark Sky, Dark Land: Stories of the Hmong Boy Scouts from Troop 100.* The students were to write a restatement and their reaction to their selected story. The Hmong writing assignment was in the form of poetry as the students can adapt this writing form into a visual image more easily than other writing assignments. Through the reading and writing opportunities the students were given a chance to learn of and share one individual's experience, sacrifice and suffering. This input to understanding the Hmong culture helped the students become more involved with the project and gave them a personal point of view to express in their art work.

The art students at our school enroll in our courses for a semester and we have required course objectives that must be taught during that semester, so to spend a vast amount of time on one stitchery project was impossible. The student assignments were based on the symbolism used by the Hmong not on the stitchery process itself. We used the Hmong symbols for two reasons. First, to teach design concepts such as symmetrical balance, positive and negative space and repetition of shape. Secondly, we selected the visual symbolic Hmong designs to gain an understanding of their meaning while viewing works of art created by the Hmong. So the art students were presented with a worksheet of Hmong symbols that have been handed down for centuries and asked to develop imagery that depicted their understanding of the Hmong culture.

The assignments that the students were involved with during this Ethnic Week project varied by the different classes. The design students created cut paper projects, using Hmong symbolism or by creating their own new symbols that depicted their understanding of symmetrical design and the Hmong culture. The printmaking students developed linoleum cuts, that created an illustration of one of the stories from *Dark Sky, Dark Land*. These illustrations were to tell of the events or personal feelings that were expressed within a selected story. The sculpture classes created three-dimensional cardboard constructions using Hmong symbols depicting their culture and its changes. The students worked using a 16" x 16" area and were to develop layers of different Hmong symbols to create negative space and a textured area. These sculptured panels were individually interesting, but also worked visually well when displayed next to each other.

We used audiotaped folktales from the Hmong to help the students become involved with another art form important to this culture. These tapes were interesting for the students to listen to while they worked on their project. The Hmong folktales were obtained from the book by Marsha MacDowell, *Stories In Thread*.

Upon the completion of all art projects, the art teachers placed student work depicting the Hmong culture on display in the library, in main hallways throughout the school, and in the individual art classrooms. This display of finished work provided the student body with a visual opportunity to begin to understand the Hmong; and this sharing process also produced a sense of pride and ownership for the students.

The art students also became sensitive to the present day existence of these people and their unbelievable adaptability which was evident in the library forums presented during Ethnic Week. The students were amazed at the young Hmong men who visited us; their command of our language, their visible inner strength and the hopes that they hold dear. Our students saw the speakers, Yee Chang and Chu Vue, as young men close to their own age, living in a new world without the support of family, past friends, and without the acceptance of their cultural traditions.

These young men did not ask for help or sympathy but were proud to tell of their past and demonstrated pride in their accomplishments since their arrival to our country. They instantly became excellent role models for all of our students in setting goals for the future.

Hmong Textile Designs

From Anthony Chan's Book *Hmong Textile Designs*

Step design and snail shell designs.

Snail shell borders and centipede design. The centipede design is highly respected for medicinal qualities.

Artist Unknown, Made in a Thailand Resettlement Camp, 8' x 8' in scale. Detailed section of Forest Scenes. Colors: lime green, yellow and pink.

Artist Unknown, 5' x 6'. Entitled, "The Flood Story." This story cloth depicts a Hmong folktale of a flood and the repopulation of the Earth.

Artist Unknown, 6' x 8' in size. Entitled, "The War." This story cloth is divided into scenes depicting the Vietnam War.

Design Motif Index

Note: The names of the designs illustrated here were primarily obtained through interviews with White Hmong women in the Lansing area. In some cases, more than one name was given for a design. Where possible, the pattern name in both Hmong and in English has been provided. Pattern name without Hmong titles were either given to us in only English or they were obtained from sources noted in the bibliography.

Corn: pobkws	Flower: paj	Scale of the fish: nptai	1. Eye of the fish: no given Hmong translation 2. Eye of the peacock: no given Hmong translation 3. Small insect: no given Hmong translation	1. Seed: noob 2. Chicken eye: muag qaib 3. Water vegetable seed: no given Hmong translation	1. Double elephant: no given Hmong translation 2. House: no given Hmong translation 3. Temple/wat (Lao Buddhist): no given Hmong translation
Cucumber vine: hmab dib	Pebble/rock: teb pob	1. Snail: kab qwj 2. "Oab qwj" design: qab qwj	Round 7: lub zeg	Starlike: no given Hmong translation	1. Rooftops: no given Hmong translation 2. Snail: no given Hmong translation 3. Tiger: trov (tus)
Vegetable blossom: paj zaub	Cucumber seed: noob dib	No English translation given: thov saws	1. Dragon: zaj 2. Rooster comb: ib qaib	Leaf frond: laug nploog suab	Snails: no given Hmong translation
					Found on the Lao flag: no given Hmong translation
Worm track: cua rab (taum laug ua)	Spider web: kab laug sab lubvas	Seed, nut: noob	Church: no given Hmong translation	Centipede-like arachnoid (indigenous to Southeast Asia): kab lij (shoo)	1. Irawhon: no given Hmong translation 2. Elephant: ntxhw (tus)
					Three-headed elephant from the royal Lao flag: no given Hmong translation
		Crab claw (in appliqué): ciaj raub ris	Tiger eyebrow: no given Hmong translation	Triangle in a triangle: nrhia	Tick (figuratively): zuam
					Ghostly hand: teg poj ntxoog
				1. "Oab qwj" design: qab qwj 2. "Snail": kab qwj	1. "Cut a path" (reverse appliqué design): tho kev
					No English translation: lub ntaub

NOTE: The Hmong Design Motif Index was compiled by Marsha MacDowell, Everyl Yankee and Annette Hafner, with assistance from Doug Gilzow, Kao Vang

Chapter 10
Following Another's Path

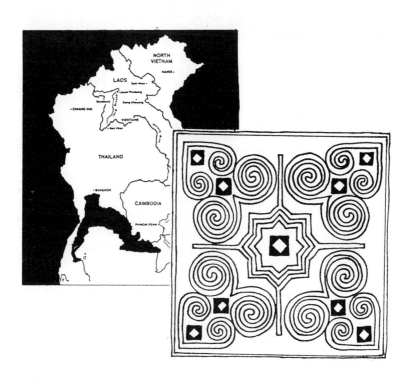

Traditional Hmong Pa Ndau
Artist Unknown, 18" x 18"
star, snail shell and tear designs

Justin Bowen, Linoleum Print

Pangu!
by Doretha Williams
(Biopoem, *World Mythology*)

The strong, hard working, self sacrificing Creator, Pangu!
Who felt the need to create a universe from chaos.
For 18,000 years he stood in fear that the sky would crush
the earth. His death gave shape to mountains, trees and formed
the planets and stars. Now he dwells within China, because he is
China.

Nugua
by Melissa Shivers
(Biopoem, *World Mythology*)

Earth Mother Goddess Nugua of the First People.
Human like, with a Dragon Tail.
Gliding across the earth.
A lover of Trees, Plants, and Flowers.
Particularly fascinated by animals and fish.

Studying them, a decision being made to finish creation.
Gliding along the Yellow River,
    Its substance forming the new human beings.
Sitting she formed handfuls of wet clay into little people.
    They looked like her, but legs replaced her tail.
Some with Yin, and others with Yang.
    Males and Females.
Nugua became tired.
    She placed a rope in the set clay.
Then picking it up, she shook it over the shore.
    Each drop, a human.
Nugua made by hand richer and more intelligent beings.
    And those who fell from the rope
Were less than others.

Overland Journey
by Dan Pound
(Found Poem, *Dark Sky, Dark Land*)

The black and white whirligigs are
A pit of empty fire
To pierce his empty stomach.
The days are long
and
Spirits of dead people
Float like dense fog
On an overland journey.

Observations
by Bill Rafferty
(Found Poem, *Dark Sky, Dark Land*)

I see helicopters landing. I am floating in a river.
Climbing out, I can see birds eating seeds.
In the shadow of darkening hills.
Our crops had been burned in the fields.
The only thing left was a house on stilts.
The sky soldiers came; and stayed.
Standing on the hills with an M-16.

The orange and yellow Mekong river flowed by.
This is my home.
Dark Sky. Dark Land.

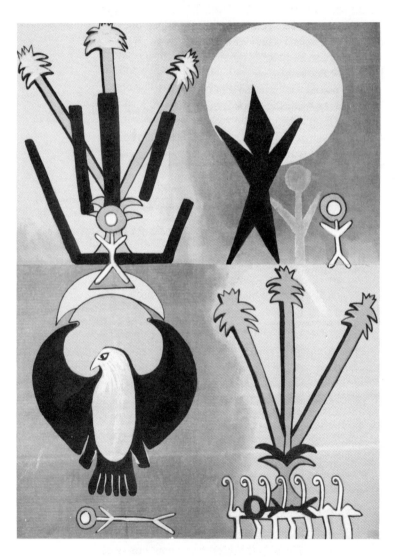

Melody Williams, Tempera Painting

Escape
by Melody Williams
(Found Poem, *Dark Sky, Dark Land*)

"Old dogs don't keep watch,"
I remember my father saying before he died.
I saw his body lying on the ground,
He looked like a little china doll.
Gunfire shattered the stillness.
So I crossed the river that was wide and black,
Hoping to start life anew.

Andrea Gisi, Cut Paper
Instructor: Royce Fleming

THUS I'AM
by Aaron Rasch
(Found Poem. *Dark Sky, Dark Land*)

THUS I'AM
village home
they made us run
river boat
refugee camp
fenced us in
escape within
fields and streams
hunt to kill
fish to eat
adventures a thrill
play again
fun and games
stop they said
school begins
not i'am
wooden tops
yes birds do sing
freedom rings
damn the man
rape again
hunger comes
hope for Americas
may come
refugee camp
freedom begins
Honolulu
hot and sun
Minnesota is my
sun
boyscouts call
THUS I'AM
friendships
begin
in Americas
Chue Hang
THUS I'AM
American

Brian Grondah, Tempera Painting

War
by Doretha Williams
(Definition. *The Killing Fields*)

War
death destruction
designed by man to be
used against many men.
Hungry for power, land, money,
people killed in cold blood, no guilt,
no shame for what they have done.
Fighting just to end up being the
only one to be
number
one.

Peace
by Doretha Williams
(Definition. *The Killings Fields*)

Peace, an idea unknown in reality. Peace will only work if everyone around the globe would do their part to make it happen. If everyone would love each other, irregardless of race, creed, wealth, or personality, the world would be one step closer to peace. Until world peace can be accomplished, we must make a peace within ourselves; spiritual peace; peace with our Lord, and peace in our soul. Some people who strive for world peace have yet to find their own peace. How can anyone love another without the love of God inside their hearts? For God is love and only God can create a perfect peace.

The Killings Fields
by Doretha Williams
(Journal, *The Killings Fields*)

The Killings Fields is a poignant film that explores Cambodia during the Vietnam War. With its graphic pictures of wounded men, women, and children and emotional scenes; this film continuously tugs at one's heart strings! My mind cannot escape the images of crying infants that were accidently left by their own families, the shocking sight of small children fighting among grown men on the battlefield, or the innocent shootings of civilians.

In so many ways, this film reminds me of the plight of the African ancestors who were brought to America. *The Killing Fields* exist as the plantations once existed. Harmless Cambodians were beaten, whipped, and murdered as were multitudes of hated Blacks. Just as the Khmer Rouge brainwashed the young Cambodians, and forced them to forget their past, so did the white man manipulate the minds of young Black Americans into thinking that their own past is insignificant. Many emotions are evoked by this film and these feelings do not fade at its conclusion. Sadness, hatred, fear, disgust run rampant in the mind. How could humans do these things to other humans? How can killing innocent children be justified or even tolerated? Will the world ever stop the mad killing, stripping people of love, peace and happiness ... life? Anger is what I might feel but the only emotions that can be offered are Love, Compassion, and Prayer for the ignorant of the world!

One can travel anywhere around the world and see the love of family and friends. No one country can isolate love and friendship to one single area. Even the tribulations of war cannot break a bonded friendship. In the movie *The Killing Fields,* Dith Pran and Sydney Schanberg form a friendship that even endures as time goes by. In the search for Pran, Schanberg convinces his conscience that his friend is still alive, even though both are worlds apart.

Christine Hathaway, Tempera Painting

Xe Yang
by Kara VanCleaf
(Interior Monologue. *Dark Sky, Dark Land*)

If the soldiers see me crying and not taking part in the execution of my fellow prisoner they will tie me up next to him and beat me to death as well. All I can do is weep. Weep for my lost family, my tortured friends, my demoralized country, my own despondent life. As I watch my friend die a sense of jealousy overcomes me. The thought of death is almost peaceful. I have not known the feeling of security or beatitude in my life. The pain, torment, and hunger I have seen and been a part of in the past eleven years is enough to last eleven lifetimes. Yet the feeling of hope overcomes all other feelings of distress. The thought of ever experiencing such wonderful and unknown feelings is reason enough to continue on strong and proud. For all of my people I must strive to fulfill the one goal of peace and happiness.

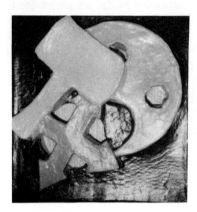

Brian Grondahl, Cardboard Construction

Cynthia Guerrero, Cut Paper
Instructor: Mike Callaway

Pan Dow
(Pa Ndau)
(A Play Inspired by the Hmong)
by Peter Wedel

This play is dedicated to my friend, Chu Vue, and to the thousands of Hmong people who lived through the terror of the war in Southeast Asia. Their lives provided an inspiration for the following story. It is through people like Chu that the world will know peace.

History has proven that my people, the Hmong people, do not forget their promises. We, the Hmong people, will never forget that America is more than the home of the free. It is the source of our freedom. We will always remember that. That is my promise to you.—Chue Vue

Characters:

ADULT LEE. Distinguished looking, middle aged Asian American
AMERICAN CHU. Lee's son, a typical American 18 year old
LEE'S MOTHER. Young, gentle, obviously loving
LEE'S GRANDMOTHER. Small, elderly peasant, with a pleasant face
LEE'S FATHER. A young man
YOUNG LEE. An eight year old boy
VANG. Lee's brother, age 10
CHU. Lee's brother, age 11
PING. Lee's brother, age 12
XI. Lee's uncle, father's brother, a very young man, also earnest
RESISTANCE LEADER
FIVE VILLAGERS
   The family, the villagers, and the Resistance Leader are costumed in traditional, simple Hmong pajamas
COMMUNIST OFFICIAL. Dressed for combat
TWO COMMUNIST SOLDIERS. Also dressed for combat

Time: 1970s during the war in Southeast Asia

Place: Briefly in America thirty years later; the mountain village in Laos where Lee was born and the surrounding jungle; the Mekong River and a refugee camp in Thailand.

The playing space is divided into two areas by a diagonal line, which runs from downstage right to upstage left. The area behind this diagonal is on short platforms and represents the hut where Lee's family lives. There is a large, black cooking pot in the center, and a large quilting frame in the far corner. The other area in front of the diagonal accommodates various places as designated at various times: the fields, the jungle, the village school, the mountains, the bank of the Mekong River, and a refugee barracks in Thailand. On the outside far right corner of the stage sit two chairs, and a table with a lamp. They are never illuminated except in Scene 1 and at the conclusion of Act III.

The convention of the staging is one of traveling through time and place. The less set there is the better. The locales should be only suggestions, and the movement from one to another should be accomplished with lights.

ACT I

Scene 1:

The stage is dark except for the far right corner where two men sit on chairs on either side of a platform lamp.

ADULT LEE: *(Addressing young man, while holding a neatly folded, unusually patterned quilt of some sort.)* They say we are a people who survive. That we are like the seeds from the grass. Scattered and growing throughout the world today. We are known to be a warrior people, strong in our resolve from the time we first left northern China to find our mountain home in Laos. You are my son and the one who will bear our family's name and history. Tomorrow you leave for college. It is time you knew all of the miracle of my existence and your own. This quilt is called "Pan Dow." It was made by your great grandmother.

AMERICAN CHU: *(interrupting)* Why haven't I ever seen it before? Where did you keep it? You never mentioned your grandmother.

ADULT LEE: The story is a painful one. Part of it is sewn into the Pan Dow. The Pan Dow is where Hmong traditionally keep their history. It is embroidered into the cloth by the skilled hands of Hmong women, and it is a holy thing. It is time you had the Pan Dow with you so that you will never forget you are Hmong. So that you will never forget the story I am about to tell. It is time you knew all of my history.

AMERICAN CHU: Painful how? I always thought that you and Mom came over with Uncle XI because you had better economic opportunities. What is your story? No one ever talks about when you were a boy.

ADULT LEE: Tonight you will hear about my childhood. And you will know why it is a story I seldom tell. While I don't want it to be forgotten, it is never remembered without pain.

The spotlight goes off the two of them and the lights go up on stage.

Scene 2:
An old Hmong woman sits cross legged at the quilting frame sewing on a colorful quilt. A young Hmong woman is bent over the large, black cooking pot stirring something. A small young boy is asleep on the floor next to the quilting frame. He begins to stir. Stage right a young Hmong man is bent over holding a hoe.

MOTHER: Awake at last, Lee!

LEE: Yes, ma'am. See you in a little while.
    Lee walks to stage right. He seems to notice some beautiful country around him. He smiles and seems content. He is eight but he seems mature. His father is apparently hoeing the soil. Lee approaches him from behind. His father turns to him.

LEE: Do you need any help father?

FATHER: As a matter of fact, I do, since your brothers are not with us today. Here. *(He hands Lee a hoe.)* Take this and work beside me.
    They begin to work. There is a short pause and then Lee begins to speak.

LEE: Where are they Papa? Why aren't they here?

FATHER: They are at school son.

LEE: What's that?

FATHER: Well, I'm not exactly sure. It was your mother's idea. But from what I hear, it's a place where you can learn about far away lands and ancient times. Best of all, people say that it will help make your brothers rich, like kings.

LEE: Really, Papa? My brothers ... kings?

FATHER: That's what I hear. But as I said, I am not certain if this is true.

LEE: Can ...

FATHER: *(Interrupts.)* Enough talking. There will be plenty of time for that at dinner. For now, let us concentrate on the work at hand. We must finish before it gets too hot.

Three young boys enter stage left.

CHU, PING, VANG: *(Calling happily.)* Hello, Mama ... Grandma.

MOTHER: Hello my sons.

CHU: When do we eat?

MOTHER: Not now! Look outside. See how your younger brother works hard beside your father. Now go!

Scene 3:
   Spotlight is on the black cooking pot. Mother, Father, Grandmother, Lee, Chu, Ping, and Vang are seated on the floor in a circle around the pot.

PING: Lee, I noticed you worked very hard today. Almost like a man.

FATHER: Ping is right. I am extremely proud to have been blessed with such a son.

MOTHER: Someday you will have your own family and tend your own fields.

LEE: Maybe. But what about school?

CHU: Ah yes ... school.

The boys chuckle to themselves.

FATHER: *(Breaking the silence.)* Well?

CHU: It wasn't what I had expected. The teacher was very young. Not much older than Ping.

VANG: and it was a little crowded.

FATHER: Ping, do you feel this way as well?

PING: What Chu says is true. I was almost as old as our teacher, but only in age. He seemed to possess much wisdom.

VANG: All together, I enjoyed it.

FATHER: God. I would not like to think that you are going there for nothing.

LEE: Were there any children there?

PING: Oh yes, there were many children.

LEE: My age?

PING: A few. Some even younger.

LEE: Papa, I would like to go there with my brothers tomorrow.

FATHER: No. Maybe in a few years, but not now.

LEE: Please Papa. I want to learn like my brothers.

CHU: It might not be a bad idea.

FATHER: No, Lee must help here at home. When all of you go there will be no one left except Lee. All of my sons have wonderful destinies. *(Points to Chu)* Chu, you will be a merchant and be rich. *(Points to Vang)* Vang, you will be a scholar and perhaps teach a school of your own. *(Points to Ping)* Ping will someday marry and give me many grandchildren. And

Lee will stay home and learn from his father how to plow a field. One day, when your Papa is too old to even stand, Lee with his own family will continue the Wong tradition and take over as master of this house.

LEE: I understand this, Papa and it seems good. But, my mind is hungry. I do not mean disrespect but I would like to go to school ...

FATHER: No disrespect?! I offer you my life and you refuse it as if it were nothing! You will not go to school, Lee! Not now or ever ... Eat your food outside away from my sight!

LEE runs off crying to stage right and sits down across the stage facing away from his family. A young Hmong man enters from the left.

XI: Greetings all!

FATHER: Hello, my brother. We weren't expecting you.

XI: Yes, well I managed to arrive early.

MOTHER: *(To boys.)* Where are your manners? Say hello to your Uncle.

One by one, PING, VANG, CHU get up and greet XI.

XI: Where's Lee?

FATHER: We had an argument. He's outside.

XI: Can I say hello to him?

FATHER: Well ...

MOTHER: *(Nudges FATHER.)* Of course you can, XI. He loves you more than life itself. Go on. Come on, Papa. Finish your dinner.

XI walks to stage right. The light follows him. He walks up to LEE slowly and without a sound LEE is lying on the ground, crying.

XI: What's the matter?

LEE turns around quickly, stunned.

LEE: Uncle XI! *(Wiping the tears from his cheeks.)* What are you doing here?

XI: I have some business to discuss with your father. But never mind that. What are you doing here. Why are you crying? *(LEE does not answer.)* Come on, you can tell me. Maybe I can help.

LEE: Well, I want to go to school but Papa won't let me. He says I have to stay here on the mountain and run the farm.

XI: *(Laughing.)* Is that all? Well, I'll see what I can do. Meanwhile, you get inside so you don't anger your father further.

LEE and XI exit to stage left. Lights dim.

Scene 4:

The setting is the same as before. There is a faint light stage left while the rest of the stage remains dark.

XI and FATHER enter.

XI: You must come.

FATHER: I don't know Xi. I'm a farmer not a soldier.

XI: Don't be stupid. Everyone will be there.

FATHER: Then they won't miss me Xi, I'm happy here. I've worked hard to have a loving family. This could take that all away.

XI: Yes it could! And it will if you don't defend yourself! This war will come to this village too, brother. And when it does where will you run? How will you live? If you join us now you might still have chance.

FATHER: I don't know. Ah! Why did this have to happen? Especially now with my sons at such a precious age.

XI: I don't know why. I don't have all the answers. All I'm saying is that I have been with the American soldiers for a year now. They treat me better than any communist. Take side now brother, while you still can.

XI begins to exit stage right. As reaches the threshold, he steps and turns toward FATHER.

XI: By the way, let Lee go to school tomorrow.

FATHER: *(Turning around in surprise.)* What? Not you too.

XI: It will be in our best interest if everyone is kept busy. Besides, school is probably the safest place for our children to be. The Communists have been known to steal sons from the fields. I'll see you tomorrow.

XI exits stage right. Spotlight on FATHER. Worried look on face. After a few seconds, spotlight goes off as the curtain closes.

ACT II

Scene 1:
Same setting as before. FATHER, LEE, MOTHER, CHU, VANG, PING are gathered stage right just outside the house area. GRANDMOTHER is still stage left working on the same quilt.

MOTHER: *(To LEE.)* Now you be careful. Listen to your brothers and pay attention. I want to know what you learned today.

LEE: *(Excited.)* Yes Mother.

Exit LEE. FATHER enters.

MOTHER: I still don't think you should go.

FATHER: I don't know. We can already hear the bombs. It can't hurt anyway.

Pause. They briefly embrace and FATHER exits stage right. Lights dim as bombs are heard in the distance.

Scene 2:

There are a few benches and chairs stage left and stage right. RESIS-TANCE LEADER stands elevated by a riser center stage. There is little commotion as lights come on. R. L. stands on a platform and calls for attention. Bombing is heard offstage.

R. L.: Listen! Some of you have been here before but for·many of you, this is a new experience. There is a war going on. Right now, it remains distant. But soon, I promise you, it will reach this village. *(Pause as bombs are heard in the distance.)* Listen, you can already hear the thunder of destruction. One day, such a storm will hang over your heads as well. And when it comes, will you be ready? When your crops are burned, what will you eat? When your houses are destroyed, where will you live? *(Pause.)* And when the communists come, where will you hide your children?

VILLAGER 1: We do not know. But what can we do?

R. L.: You can defend yourself. All of you. You can all stand up and refuse to let your lives be taken from you.

VILLAGER 2 stands up.

VILLAGER 2: But how? We do not know such things. Look around, you see no weapons. Ever since our ancestors fled from China, this has been a peaceful village. How can we farmers suddenly become soldiers?

R. L.: I am glad that you have asked that question for that is the reason why I am here. There is a Hmong general, a great leader who is helping the Americans in Laos. This general, General Vang Pao, has been a great force against the Communist army. Under his command, you will be trained for combat and be issued military equipment. If you decide to join, you and your family will be taken care of in cases of wartime losses. Anyone over 16 may enlist.

The VILLAGERS discuss this among themselves. Slowly they begin to go to a table up center stage where a man in uniform is seated. They give their names to him and exit stage down stage left. The spotlight is on XI and FATHER who are standing among the villagers.
XI and FATHER have a discussion. FATHER seems to be contemplating the decision.

XI: Come on. For the family. For the future.

FATHER: All right, all right.

They move toward the table as lights dim.

Scene 3:
FATHER, MOTHER, CHU, VANG, PING, GRANDMOTHER, XI are sitting around the large cooking pot.

MOTHER: So how was school, Lee?

LEE: Different. It was somewhat hard. Like doing field work only with words and numbers.

MOTHER: And the rest of you?

CHU: The same.

VANG: No difference.

PING: Lee is an excellent student.

CHU: He answered many questions.

VANG: The teacher complimented him.

MOTHER: *(Very pleased.)* Really?

FATHER: Enough! Enough talk of school!

FATHER gets up and walks to down stage left. The others look stunned and then pretend to not notice him. MOTHER follows.

MOTHER: What's the matter?

FATHER: I am joining the resistance as XI has.

MOTHER: *(Anguished.)* No!

FATHER: I'm not sure if it is right, but the war is real. Listen ... it's coming.

Bombs are heard offstage. Louder than they have been before.

Scene 4:

Lights are up full. FATHER, LEE, PING, VANG, CHU, stage right on field. MOTHER stands stage left. Sounds of airplanes and gunfire can be heard clearly. All look to the skies. Bombs sound very loudly. Strobe light is added. FATHER, CHU, VANG, PING, XI all fall to the ground as bomb "hits." LEE is left standing in center stage. Another bomb hits and MOTHER jumps and falls. LEE screams. Lights dim.

Scene 5:

All of the family except MOTHER sits on the center stage on the floor in a semi-circle facing the audience. The lights are dimmed except for a special focused on the family.

FATHER: With your mother's death, I have decided to fight the communists.

PING, CHU, VANG, LEE: *(Frightened.)* Papa, wait....

FATHER: Now listen! You will stay here and help Uncle XI and the others restore our village.

LEE: Don't go Papa. Out there is death, like Mama. We can't survive without you.

FATHER: I'll be back, don't worry.

VANG: And if not?

Pause.

XI: If not then Xi will take care of you. No more harm will come to you boys, I promise.

FATHER stands up and takes a staff, and a cloth tied to hold a few possessions. Children stand up as well.

FATHER: *(Voice breaks.)* Well, I must be off. *(He embraces each boy in turn very tightly.)*

FATHER exits stage right. Lights dim.

Scene 6:
VILLAGERS are quietly talking. COMMUNIST OFFICIAL stands on platform. TWO soldiers are seated on either side of the speaker. All are quiet.

COMMUNIST: Gentlemen and elders of this village. I am pleased to announce that the war is over. *(The villagers chatter in bewilderment.)* There are still a few renegades who refuse to give up. Therefore, we have been assigned her to keep peace in this village. Any questions? *(Hands go up. COMMUNIST ignores them.)* Good. If there are none, then I must ask all of you to line up and proceed to the table behind me. You will answer a series of questions to the best of your abilities. And remember ... this is for posterity so please, be honest.

COMMUNIST OFFICIAL begins to leave. VILLAGER 1 stands up.

VILLAGER 1: And what if we refuse?

TWO SOLDIERS cock their guns in unison at this comment. COMMUNIST OFFICIAL stops and turns around.

COMMUNIST: I don't think you want me to answer that. *(He walks off but suddenly stops.)* By the way, is there a Xi present? Xi? *(XI proudly steps forward.)* I wish to speak with you in private.

XI and COMMUNIST walk to down stage left. Lights darken on rest of the stage. Special light comes up on the two men.) My superiors have been watching you and they feel that you are best suited to be leader of this village. You are intelligent and physically formidable which makes you perfect. I trust you will accept this with responsibility and honor.

XI thinks it over.

XI: Yes sir.

COMMUNIST: *(Laughing.)* Good, you are a wise man. Meet me here tomorrow at noon. Now if you will excuse me, I must get back to business.

COMMUNIST exits stage right as lights dim.

Scene 7:
Special on GRANDMOTHER, who is sewing carefully on the brightly colored quilt. LEE enters from off stage left.

LEE; What does that mean Grandma? The colors and pictures? I've seen you working on it but you've never told me.

GRANDMA: Ah, it is good that you ask. You are growing up to be a fine man, Lee. I am very proud.

LEE: *(Embarrassed but obviously pleased.)* Thank you, Grandma.

GRANDMOTHER: As for you question, here is the answer. This is called Pan Dow, my child. It is an ancient craft passed down from our ancestors. But it is much more than simple thread you see. Within these stiches lie the suffering and joy of our people. It is our past, it is our present, it is our future. Many years ago our people were forced to leave their home in China. Today, I fear that the pattern continues. Death grows near and soon we must run.

LEE: But Papa....

XI enters in a hurry from stage left with CHU, PING and Vang. As XI speaks, lights come up on entire left stage. LEE remains still.

XI: Hurry! We must take what we can!

LEE: Why?!

XI: We leave tonight!

LEE has a puzzled look on his face. GRANDMOTHER stops her work on the Pan Dow.

LEE: But why?

XI: Enough talk! Just take what you can easily carry! *(LEE is puzzled.)* I'm sorry. The communists have won, or so they say. Today at the meeting they named me leader of the village. They may not have discovered my connection with the Resistance and Americans. But they soon will. I will not do the Communists' bidding.

LEE: Why not refuse?

XI: And be shot? Do you wish to become a communist slave? No thank you. That is why we must leave tonight. They are leaving but they will return at sunrise. Now hurry!

   Lights dim.

ACT III

Scene 1:
There is a white screen placed a few feet from back stage. FIVE VILLAGERS run back and forth behind this screen. Blue lights illuminate the stage, also behind the screen. This way only silhouettes are seen. XI, GRANDMOTHER, LEE, CHU, VANG, PING are placed in front of screen. A blue strobe light is placed downstage. Sounds of gunfire and bombs offstage. PING carries GRANDMOTHER on his back. After a few seconds, the lights dim and then rise. The family enters from stage right. GRANDMOTHER and boys rest down stage right. XI takes PING downstage left. Lights are dim on stage right. Special on XI and PING.

XI: I can see that you are tired from carrying Grandma.

PING: Yes, she is heavy.

XI: I know. *(Pauses and bows his head.)* She slows us down. How can we survive with the communists at our heels? We will all die quickly if we cannot escape.

   PING leaves to stage right to join the others. Lights follow him. He whispers to LEE and LEE begins to cry. All move towards GRAND-MOTHER who is isolated stage right. Lights come up on this area. XI tries to speak but GRANDMOTHER interrupts.

GRANDMOTHER: Do not speak. Your tongue may betray you. I have come as far as I will go. I know that you have plans to leave Laos, but I will not go with you. I was born here and here I will die. Now leave me, all of you. You have a long way to go and the river is not far. *(They all begin to exit stage left. LEE drags behind.)* Lee wait. *(LEE turns around. Lights are dimmed except for a special focused upon LEE and GRAND-MOTHER.)* I have something for you. *(She brings out the Pan Dow from under her shirt.)*

LEE: Grandma, your Pan Dow! I can't accept that.

GRANDMOTHER: Nonsense! What good will it do here but die with its maker? Take it with you into the new land. Never forget its secrets. Only through the Pan Dow can the Hmong be free. For us the Pan Dow is a sacred thing. (LEE begins to cry.) Now go. Quickly. *(LEE hugs his GRANDMOTHER and then runs off stage left. Light remains on GRAND-MOTHER and then dims.)*

Scene 2:
   The stage is empty. Fog lies low on stage. XI, LEE, CHU, VANG, PING enter stage left.

XI: Here we are at last! The river is wide, but we will cross it to Thailand and freedom.

LEE: And what of Papa?

PING: We're not going to see him again are we?

   All except XI hang their heads. After a long pause, VAN speaks.

VANG: *(Sobbing.)* Why did he have to fight?!

XI: *(Surprised, defensive.)* He fights so that you may have a better life. So that you may be free. He realizes that we have run long enough. Do not cry boys. Your father is a fine man and likewise, you are fine children. *(The brothers hold their heads up now.)*

CHU: Is Papa dead?

XI: I don't know. But I promised him I would watch out for you when he left. He did not know I would have to take you but we must cross this river. On the other side is freedom. Now come! Be brave. We must cross before sunrise.

All exit stage right to the sounds of gunfire and bombs. Lights dim.

Scene 3:
   LEE enters from stage left, alone. A thick fog drifts across the stage. he appears lost. All lights are dimmed except a special on LEE. He is holding the Pan Dow.

LEE: Father? Mother? Where are you? I can't see you.

   FATHER, MOTHER, GRANDMOTHER are illuminated to the front right of LEE. They are wearing traditional Hmong dress. Dozens of little silver "metals" are hanging from FATHER'S shirt. They make a tinkling sound with each movement. MOTHER wears many silver necklaces, as does GRANDMOTHER. Their clothing glitters in the light.

FATHER, MOTHER: Here we are Lee. Where we've always been.

LEE: Why did you leave? Why?

MOTHER: We have never left you. Our blood flows with yours. We are one.

FATHER: You were right to want to learn Lee. You were right to want to be free. Someday, you will have a family and a home in a new land. There you can stop running. Now stop crying. You will be a fine man. We will always be here. All of us.

   XI, CHU, VANG, PING enter and stand together on stage around LEE.

GRANDMOTHER: Never forget that we are kept alive in the story told in the Pan Dow.

   A gong sounds as the lights go out on stage and a spot goes on the far right corner where once again ADULT LEE and AMERICAN CHU are sitting.

ADULT LEE: And so I pass our story on to you.

He reverently passes the Pan Dow over to AMERICAN CHU who bows his head. The light dims as the curtain falls.

THE END

Michael Larkin

Kerri Neufeld

Dan Fager

Chapter 11
Cobblestones for New Paths

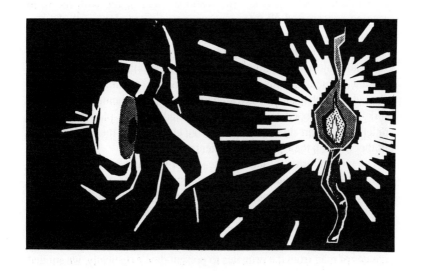

Cory Wilson, Computer Graphics

Vitalistic Human

This chapter represents a new twist in developing a cultural study for us. The purpose of the next project, which we entitled "Vitalistic Human" was to provide our students with an additional cultural activity other than what was available through our Ethnic Week activities which previously originated with the library. The library involvement was equally important with this project; however, our approach to this new undertaking was vastly different.

The "Vitalistic Human" project was an across the curriculum, multi-faceted educational opportunity involving art, science, and creative writing students. We also incorporated the school's computer lab as the sounding board for the students to use in expressing their educational experiences. The students involved with this project were enrolled in advanced placement biology, studio art, commercial design, or survey of the fine arts. The teachers involved with implementing this project were Linda Wiley, one of our science teachers; Theresa Steinlage, creative writing teacher and facilitator of the computer lab during the hours that we worked on this project, and Lynda Miller, an art teacher. As with the other Ethnic Week activities, the workload was shared with the team teaching concept and all three teachers participated along with the students to develop work that could be shared with one another. The teachers did not ask the students to do work that they themselves were not doing. Our main objective in putting these students together was to make our talented science students more creative and to encourage our visually talented art students to use investigative research in planning their visual work. We developed teams among the students that placed a science student with an art student for variety, but also to allow them to assist one another through their given assignments.

The project lasted throughout the school year and involved two completely different studies (one each semester). The time frame for each project lasted approximately seven class periods, plus additional study time outside of class to complete the assigned work.

During the first semester, we explored the development or evolution of man in body, mind, and spirit. Scientifically, we studied the physical body changes of man from the primates to present day. Artistically, we studied the symbols and beliefs of man and developed computer generated images in the computer lab at Topeka West High School. In creative writing we wrote in narrative and in poetry about the changes of man in body, mind and spirit from prehistoric time to the present day.

Our major objectives during this project were to connect unrelated units of study together in order to create new interests in learning; to force new connections in how mankind has developed in physical, mental, and spiritual areas; and to provide the students with higher levels of thinking and to encourage students to react and present their learning in different ways. We also wanted to create a team-teaching experience that would provide students computer time that involved both word processing as well as a graphic experience.

The research, art work, and creative writing were evaluated by all three instructors in their area of expertise. Each student also was provided with an opportunity to evaluate this project with our special day of sharing provided in the library. The student reactions to this project basically stated that they thought the project was interesting, hard, but very worthwhile.

The "Vitalistic Human" project for first semester was an exploration of past cultures or cultures that have influenced all existing cultures today, but that now no longer exist. Each of the three teachers lectured about the timeline of prehistoric to present day; one spoke to the physical changes of man, one addressed the spiritual changes of man, and last but not least, one teacher lectured on the intellectual changes of man. The specific student assignment for our first semester project was to compare man's physical evolution to the evolution of the mind and spirit. Each student was assigned a partner and they were to agree on a common topic to study. Each student was responsible for his or her own work for both the research portion and for the assigned final product. Team members were to work together to research, discuss, and brainstorm ideas, but in the end, each individual was to turn in the following materials: the factual research concerning the topic, an accumulated vocabulary list, a sketch page of visual symbols relating to the selected culture, and the final project. This project was a poem, a narrative writing, and a computer-generated visual. The students received worksheets on how to write their poems and an explanation of the narrative writing assignment. They received instructions on how to document their research and received computer instruction on word processing and the use of our graphics program available in the computer lab. Three days of computer time was provided and the computer lab was available for the students before and after school any time during our study.

A Cultural Mosaic

To assist the students in developing their projects we scheduled one day for the students to do research in the library. Also a library cart full of a vast variety of resources was gathered together for the students to use in the computer lab. These books were assembled by the librarians and they also were available in the library for students who needed additional assistance any time throughout this project.

Upon the completion of all projects, we placed the student work into a book which was given to each student. We had a book signing party in the library and the students took turns reading their work.

Our second semester project was designed to be a study of existing cultures of the students' individual choices. Once again we wanted to provide our students with an opportunity to broaden their understanding of the cultural diversity within their midst. The one major difference in this project over our other cultural studies was that the students were to pick their own culture to study. There were thirty students involved in this project, and our librarians developed a cart of books covering approximately forty-five known cultures from which the students could select. No culture could be used for this study more than once, so upon the completion of this project, we would all learn about thirty different cultures which exist today.

After the students had selected their culture, they had to do research, complete a writing, and develop a visual aid to use in speaking about this culture on our sharing day. Each student was to develop a 12" x 12" square painted panel located on a large 4' x 8' board. In this panel, the students were to react through their painting to variations in body, environment, traditions, art forms, rituals, beliefs, customs, costumes, and any other significant information which would help them teach their fellow students about their selected culture. Many of the students also incorporated their creative writing into their assigned panel.

Our sharing day was scheduled in the library, refreshments were served, and each student was provided with two minutes of classtime to share information about their selected culture. Each student demonstrated respect, understanding and appreciation for their selected culture. This project was very rewarding for all involved and will be continued in the future. Note the photograph of this large visual board entitled "A Cultural Mosaic."

The following poem was written by the three sponsors of this project as a teaching aid.

Vitalistic Human

To know another you must
    walk with him
        know his emotions:
            his pains, his joys, his sorrows.

To know is not to judge another by heresay, it is to
    accept diversity with knowledge and compassion.

To know is to walk in another's shoes,
    to have felt his pain, joy and sorrow.

To know is to see the beauty of his world,
    by feeling his space and studying his art forms.

It is to know that we are all one in body, mind and spirit,
    and in judging another, we judge ourselves.

From Dust 'Till Now
by Christine Hathaway

Try to remember ...
where did it start?
God was hidden
walking
hunting for meaning
... arrived the Leader
much land has been covered
much else expanded
Now there is no time to ponder
all is rushed
only look to the future
the past is uncontrollable.

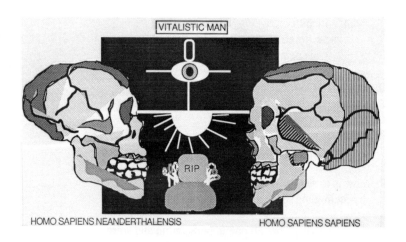

Rachael Chan, Computer Graphics

Lucy
by Richard Sanchez

Broken bones
in the desert sun
found in the dirt

A song in the air
was your name.

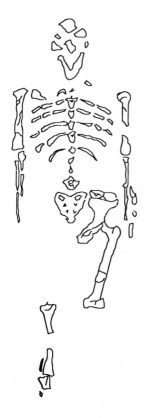

Richard Sanchez, Computer Graphics

Jennifer Chang, Computer Graphics

Eve of Day
by Jennifer Chang

I watch the moon white glow
Beaming beauty and wisdom
Across the frozen plains.
My face scarred with dirt,
my face blackened by the soot of fire
is not of celestial lunar beauty
but of my earthbound hunt for survival

This is the Time
(1150 A.D.)
by Jason A. Turner

This is the time of struggle and strife,
I hide inside to save my life.
For out those doors in the dark of the night
Are demons, I know for my soul they will fight.

And if I escape them I know I will flee
And the farther I go the more I will bleed
For at the end of my journey
The end of the earth will send me burning

These are the times of struggle and strife
I hide inside to save my life
The knights in their quarters
Protect our borders
From the witch that lives beyond our castle walls
And the wizard, the dragon he calls

I will find peace soon very soon
For the clergy-man comes here to save at high noon
He talks of new time, the time of the church
When Christianity will sit on its perch

This is the time of struggle and strife
I hide inside to save my life
Sitting here searching, just hoping to find
My peace, my peace that will come in time

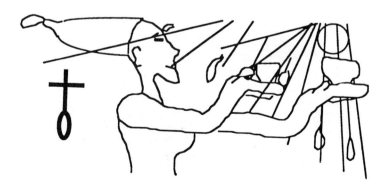

Jeremy Turner, Computer Graphics

Roman
by Kate Gilliland

I woke this evening
    scared, wondering
It is May, Lemuria, when spirits come.
    Tonight at midnight
I must send the lemures
    back to the Underworld.
I have to protect my family
    from these evil spirits.
I am now Head of the Household.
All responsibilities are mine.
    I pray to Pluto
    to take these spirits
    back to his realm,
    take them back to Tartarus,
    their place of punishment.
I pray to Porserpine
    Queen of the Underworld
    to take these spirits back.
I pray to the Gods to protect my family.
With the ritual I will send these spirits
    back to their realm.
The gods protect me and mine.

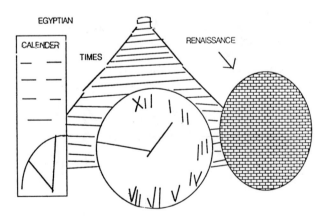

Kim Massek, Computer Graphics

The Serf
by Jennifer McLaughlin

History whispers between its documented lines.
About my ancestors' life, quite different from mine.
Dust clinging to your sandals worn.
Wearily trudging to the central dipping water well.
You greet the early morning dawn,
your day long duty—endless
labor—just began.

The chores did quickly mar the smooth, soft skin of the child.
Harsh sun's rays etched their marks in your face.
Yet the gentleness was still found in the touch of your
rough, calloused hands.
Did those hands start to hurt and tire, before the day began?
And in those moments, did you find it hard to go silently and
Pray to Nector, your Supreme God?

When the desert sky tinged with pink,
Signaling the chattering of the dog-headed ape gods to
Reassure you that today will be a good day,
Did you find it hard to believe them?

And when the blistered wind drove the heat to evaporate
Your precious water,
Did you in desperation, turn to meet the graven image of Hepi?

You were good, I know.
Always obeying and praying with a loving heart,
Your deeds on your death to Osiris show he would judge you
Well.
And with the blessed ones in after life, you will dwell.

Christine Hathaway, Computer Graphics

A Conversation with a Student of Plato's Academy
(DIALOG Assignment)
by Mike Kauffman

The wonders of modern technology have provided me with an extraordinary opportunity to speak with people of the past. The following is an excerpt from my interview with a student at Plato's Academy in Ancient Greece. I chose to speak with a student of Plato's rather than Plato himself so I could get a more accurate sense of the times from the perspective of someone not unlike myself: a student.

Mike: I would like to thank you for agreeing to allow me to speak with you. I feel that it will be most helpful and insightful to speak with someone like yourself.

Lyrus: It is my pleasure to speak with you. There have been others who have made the trip to speak with people from this time, but they have only expressed interest in men like Plato and Aristotle. I feel that I will be able to give you an insight they cannot.

Mike: That is what I hoped, but what exactly do you mean?

Lyrus: Plato and Aristotle are diametrically opposed in the vast majority of their views on the world. Plato learned from Socrates and Aristotle has just recently left this Academy after learning from Plato. Plato and Socrates are, for all practical purposes, identical. Plato and Aristotle are not. I feel this comes from the fact that Aristotle was of a different mold. Plato was the world's greatest rationalist. He believed in metaphysics on a grand scale; things such as a supreme order, ideal forms, and that the world around us is nothing more than a poor imitation of an ideal world. He was not a mechanical thinker in the sense that "a" leads to "b." He thought in terms of the abstract and the absolute. Aristotle, on the other hand, discredited Plato's concepts of the abstract in favor of observation and analysis. He studied everything there is to study. He did more to advance the beginnings of modern science than any person before him.

Mike: I find that interesting. I had always thought that since Plato taught Aristotle they might be more similar in their beliefs. I guess that because the history of Greece was never stressed during my education in the American Public School System that I really never learned enough about the philosophy of the two to realize that they were so different.

Lyrus: You mentioned your school education being somewhat lacking. What was it like?

Mike: They try to educate you in the basics such as math, science, English, and history, but the problem is that expectations are low and exceptional work is not rewarded as it should be. People get by whether they do nothing or all they can do. As a result, too many people choose to do nothing. What was life at the Academy like?

Lyrus: The education I have received is phenomenal. I have learned from a master on subjects ranging from the arts and sciences to physical education. I have learned the most current information available as well as how life used to be and have been allowed to see the reasons it has changed. I can think of no better place to be.

Mike: What is life outside of school like? The impression I have received is that everyone is a thinker who spends their time walking about pondering the meaning of life.

Lyrus: Nothing could be further from the truth. Very few people are philosophers like Plato, Aristotle, and myself. In fact, the people of Athens do not appreciate Plato or Aristotle. That is why Socrates was murdered. The "leaders" of Athens felt he was a danger to their existence. The same goes for Plato. Although he has not been murdered, the aristocracy is afraid of him because he questioned their democratic system. He challenged the system. His ideas and followers wanted to take away the hold because many people in later years thought he was responsible for democracy. Not true. He proposed a system ruled by one man, a philosopher king. Anyway, I digress. There are other reasons for the problems in Athens. There is great division between the city-states and even within each one. Athens and Sparta are the leaders, but there is conflict between them and within their walls. The reason for the internal conflict is the great separation between the upper and middle classes. There are also a number of slaves and wealth is held only by the aristocracy. It is not the perfect world you might think. Time seems to make problems disappear. It is obvious that time has made historians forget exactly what life was like here in Athens.

Mike: Your belief in numerous gods had a strong impact upon your life. Most people in our society who believe in the existence of God believe in only one. Where do you feel the attitude changed and why?

Lyrus: One would have to point towards the birth of Jesus Christ, much after my time, as the emergence of wide-scale monotheism and the belief was that the universe crated the gods and not that the gods created the universe. This is a key difference and explains why we had numerous gods. The universe created a god to rule over all major things such as the city, the underworld, the seas, marriage, and war to name a few. We built cities around buildings to these gods. They were very instrumental in our system. I am not to say whether or not one god is better than many gods or vice versa. It is a matter of personal belief.

Mike: From what you know of the history of the world since the fall of Ancient Greece, what do you have to say about mankind.

Lyrus: I have not been able to see all that has occurred from my position now, but I do know of the basic occurrences. I would have to say that mankind is remarkably unchanged. Each succeeding generation has taken that which was left to it and built on it. Sometimes for better, sometimes for worse, but that is only natural. Progress, if you believe in it, does not always make the world a better place in which to live. Man has really changed very little. Your generation is a little taller, has a longer life expectancy and is more literate than mine, but is no more intelligent on the whole. You simply have more resources to draw upon than us. We were trend setters. We were among the first people to settle within an urban environment and were not dependent primarily on an agricultural economy. All that has occurred is simply building upon those ideas which already existed.

Mike: I have to agree with you. Change does not occur within man in a sudden burst. Change results from the slow culmination of existing ideas combined with new resources and innovation. I must say that we really are unchanged as a being in the last two thousand years.

Lyrus: I agree completely. I imagine that at some time man may change in a significant way, but that may be more out of the result of a technological innovation such as the ability to produce a superior bred of humans.

Mike: Thank you for your time, Lyrus. I appreciate your cooperation.

Lyrus: You are more than welcome.

Sarah Davis, Computer Graphics

Stone Age vs. Modern Medicine
by Justin Bowen

Ignorance
Filth
Disease
Death
Past, Present, Future.

Intelligence
Discoveries
Clean
Healthy
Present and Future.

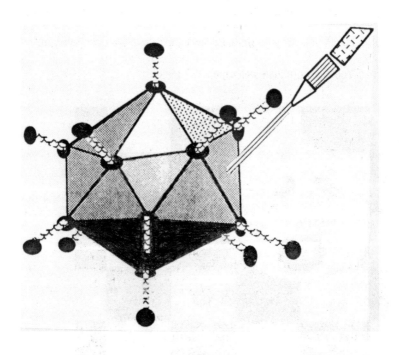

Justin Bowen, Computer Graphics

Conclusion
The Discovery of the Path

The Renaissance
by Emily Eakes

The still told story, a modern Europe,
Deep truth searched out
Focusing on education and invention,
Posterity in Harmonious unity,
A break with the old,
Traditions redefined,
We look to the future and see
A bright tomorrow,
Intelligence and creativity released
To be brought about
For generations,
Proof that change leads to prosperity.

Emily Eakes, Computer Graphics

This book is about what happened at Topeka West High School during 1988-1992 school years of a program which was born out of a need to educate ourselves and our students about the changing world in which we live. We exist within a society which is rapidly becoming more and more diverse. The traditional canon which directed our curriculums in the past simply will not meet the needs of students and teachers who are living daily in a multicultural society and a rapidly shrinking world. As early as 1977 Robert L. Williams wrote in the book *Cross-Cultural Education: Teaching Toward a Planetary Perspective,* that "A polycultural curriculum is defined as a set of prescribed student experiences provided through the school and world communities." The four Ethnic Week cultural studies and also the two "Vitalistic Human" projects were designed with this in mind. We believe they were successful in enriching the awareness of not only our students but also our school's staff, parents, and the greater Topeka community.

Yet these programs are only a beginning for us. In the complexity of the world around us and, in fact, in the complexity of our own student population, there are remarkable opportunities for future explorations. In the past we have developed our programs upon the availability of good literature depicting other cultures. Happily, as the demand for a more diverse literature increases, we will be able to approach additional projects more readily as the thrust in multicultural education continues to move to the forefront in education. Each day additional books become available that will work well in teaching understanding of our many cultures.

Our students have been an inspiration as we have tried to meet their needs. They have responded with sensitivity and insight which is remarkable. We think their work which is included in this book is a reflection of their ability to empathize and understand at a level which is what we would have wanted and more. It is important to note that in gaining this sensitivity and insight, the traditional curriculums of art, language arts, social studies, and science did not have to be compromised in any way. In fact, these curriculums were enriched as our integrated approach to teaching was implemented. Observations regarding the benefits of this approach include:

1. Students have become more aware, open-minded, compassionate, and appreciative, of the diversities within our society.
2. The variety of presentations and learning activities have provided students with opportunities to demonstrate sensitivity to the differences of humans throughout the ages.

3. Students have been made to understand their responsibilities as citizens of a quickly changing nation and world.
4. Students have discovered their individual voices and mediums for communicating that responsibility.
5. Through continued use of the library, students now know how to seek out information to grasp a better understanding of personal, community, and global concerns about a given topic.
6. Perhaps most importantly, students have witnessed first-hand through our speakers and library forums the lives, trials, triumphs and current concerns of the cultures studied.

The barebones ideas for future projects will begin through reading professional book reviews in the area of multicultural education, and through our own heightened sensitivity to materials that are already available. Future projects will also be developed through staff brainstorming sessions (which usually take place in the early morning hours in the library reference room), through tuning into the people who have knowledge or experiences to share and who are available within our community, and through familiarization with the video resources and activities that students can use to gain further understanding of a given culture. All of our future projects will revolve around a common knowledge base. However, we will continually develop other avenues or pathways for each unit studied. Some ideas to consider include:

1. Have students seek out individuals of distinction from a culture other than their own in the Topeka area and then write and/or video tape oral histories of these individuals.
2. Complete a cultural study based on a specific location or place of significance to the community. For example, a church, park, or home which is a land mark or which is noted for its historical significance. Sumner Elementary School, which was the focus of the landmark *Brown vs. The Topeka Board of Education* Supreme Court decision, would be such a place for those of us living and teaching in Topeka. However, every community has such locations; we only need to become sensitive to their existence.
3. Develop a study of agism.
4. Develop a cross-generational study with the intended objective of understanding the diversities that occur by the timeline given to us with our birth.

5. Develop a culture study focused upon the theme of folklore with each student in a given class selecting their own culture to share.

Whatever our future holds it will be important to continue these programs and to provide variety in format for the staff and students to continue to want to take part.

Our belief is that we should always teach students that *all* knowledge is born of culture and that all cultures reflect the values of the people who create them. It is also our goal that our students understand that they are citizens of a diverse society formed of many cultures. And that through active participation in learning about others, they may come to an understanding that racial and cultural diversity is, in fact, an opportunity for intellectual and spiritual enrichment, as well as our greatest strength as a school, community, state, and nation formed of many different peoples.

A Word of Thanks

Our librarians, Diane Goheen and Mike Printz deserve special recognition as they have provided excellent leadership, resources, support, as well as opening the library doors to guarantee the success of these programs. It was Diane and Mike who invited us as a staff to team teach in the library during these Ethnic Week forums. This moved us from teaching in isolation to working together to teach our respective disciplines to students enrolled in one another's classes whom we may never have had the opportunity to work with otherwise. Thus our subjects were linked together to enhance each other and provide students with a richer learning opportunity. Diane and Mike are more than dedicated and have been our line to speakers, and the best possible programming. Their many hours of planning and organizational skills are greatly appreciated.

These programs would not have been possible without the support of the district and school administrations, the Topeka community, and parents of the Topeka West Booster Club. They not only provided financial backing for many of our activities, but also donated countless hours of volunteer time in organizing library packets, transportation for speakers, and on occasion even provided lodging for our guests. They are an example for other parent groups interested in supporting a quality education for their children.

Other members of our staff also deserve credit for their efforts to pull together and implement the necessary instruction and student development for each cultural study.

And special thanks to our students who daily provide us with inspiration, and whose generosity of spirit, and openness to learning from these programs may be witnessed in their work and in our continued enthusiasm.

Catalog of Student Work

Introduction:
  Stacey Nodolf, Pen and Ink
  Jennifer Somers, Found Poetry

Chapter 2
  Mark Levy, Computer Graphics

Chapter 3
  Hilary Porterfield, Line Drawing

Chapter 4
  Christi Furnas, Pen and Ink
  Jason Gilbert, Linoleum Print
  Josh Shuart, Essay
  Natalie Martin, Pastels
  Kara Van Cleaf, Biopoem
  Wendy Whiteside, Biopoem
  Larry Morford, Acrylic Painting
  Michael Book, Biopoem
  Kate Gilliland, Autobiographical Map
  Jennifer Stephens, Free Verse
  Heather Nolte, Aquatint
  Katharine Humphrey, Biopoem
  Shawn Martin, Aquatint
  Chris Bloxsom, Found Poem
  Chanee Livingston, Found Poem
  Emily Eakes, Pen and Ink
  Grey Thayer, Journal Entries

Chapter 6
  Scott Ramser, Linoleum
  Melissa Shivers, Character Poem
  Emily Eakes, Monoprint
  Jennifer Zibell, Photographic Poem .
  Katharine Humphrey, Letters
  Mary Nall, Monoprint
  Jenny Moerer, Journal

Rachael Chan, Pen and Ink
Rachael Chan, Short Story
Tracie Niles, Calliograph Print
Jennifer Zibell, Poem
John Blosser, Found Poem
Spencer Duncan, Essay

Chapter 7
Shawn Miller, Pen and Ink

Chapter 8
Robyn Butterfield, Pen and Ink
Jerad Widman, Found Poem
Jennifer Orr, Found Poem
Jason Taliaferro, Mixed Media
Tim Fisher, Nature Poetry
Tim Bruce, Found Poem
Tim Bruce, Mixed Media
Alex Burtin, Found Poem
Alex Burtin, Mixed Media
Wendy Whiteside, Chant Poem
Jennifer Long, Concrete Poetry
Tricia Quinn, Found Poem
Brent Venis, Found Poem
Lynette Grandstaff, Tempera Painting
Stacey Nodolf, Pen and Ink
Megan Botsford, Concrete Poetry
Eleanor Turner, Concrete Poetry
Christy Shaffer, Pen and Ink
Greg Thayer, Short Story
Shawn Miller, Tempera Painting

Chapter 9
Emily Eakes, Linoleum Print

Chapter 10
Justin Bowen, Linoleum Print
Dan Pound, Found Poem
Melissa Shivers, Biopoem
Doretha Williams, Biopoem

Melody Williams, Tempera Painting
Bill Rafferty, Found Poem
Melody Williams, Found Poem
Andrea Gisi, Cut Paper
Aaron Rasch, Found Poem
Brian Grondahl, Tempera
Doretha Williams, Definition Poems
Doretha Williams, Journal Entries
Christine Hathaway, Tempera Painting
Brian Grondahl, Cardboard Construction
Kara Van Cleaf, Interior Monologue
Cynthia Guerrero, Cut Paper
Peter Wedel, Play
Michael Larkin, Cardboard Construction
Kerri Neufeld, Cardboard Construction
Dan Fager, Cardboard Construction

Chapter 11
Cory Wilson, Computer Graphics
Rachael Chan, Computer Graphics
Christine Hathaway, Computer Graphics
Richard Sanchez, Computer Graphics
Richard Sanchez, Poem
Jennifer Chang, Computer Graphics
Jeremy Turner, Computer Graphics
Jason Turner, Poem
Kim Massek, Computer Graphics
Kate Gilliland, Poem
Jennifer McLaughlin, Poem
Christine Hathaway, Computer Graphics
Mike Kauffman, Dialog
Sarah Davis, Computer Graphics
Justin Bowen, Computer Graphics
Justin Bowen, Poem

Conclusion
Emily Eakes, Computer Graphics
Emily Eakes, Poem

Appendix
   Doug Wagner, Computer Graphics
   James Newman, Pen and Ink
   Karli Pigg, Cut Paper

Appendix
Signposts

**Library Media Center Project Handouts
for Ethnic Week Activities 1989-1992
Topeka West High School**

We've Come So Far

I look to the past and see,
just how far we've come.
From such primal thinking,
to voyages into the realms of space.
Once we thought the stars
were the gods above.
Now we travel by our own
means to those very stars.
Our ancestors roamed the earth,
now we roam free over the galaxy.
Never would anyone have believed,
we could become so adept.
To conquer the universe,
to be the knowledge of generations.
What happened to cause
this miracle called Man.

Doug Wagner

Lynda Miller

TOPEKA WEST HIGH SCHOOL LIBRARY

PRESENTS

ETHNIC WEEK 1989

March 6-10, 1989

SOMEHOW TENDERNESS SURVIVES
Apartheid in South Africa

Purpose

The goal of the Ethnic Week activities at Topeka West High School is
to raise the awareness of students and staff members concerning Apartheid
(pronounced "a-part-hate") in South Africa.

I have cherished the ideal of a democratic and free society in
which all persons live together in harmony and with equal
opportunities. It is an ideal which I hope to live for and to achieve.
But if needs be, it is an ideal for which I am prepared to die.

Nelson Mandela
Leader, African National Congress
Sentenced to life in prison, 1964

Library Forums

On Monday, March 6, 1989, Prexy Nesbitt, Executive Director, Chicago Committee for Solidarity in South Africa, will speak to several classes in the library during 1st, 2nd, and 3rd hours.

On Tuesday, March 7, 1989, Rob Jones, Projects Director, American Committee on Africa, New York, will speak to several classes in the library during 1st, 2nd, 3rd, 5th, and 6th hours.

If teachers are interested in bringing your classes to these forums, contact Diane Goheen or Mike Printz in the library.

Exhibits

Apartheid Art Exhibit: Lynda Miller's art students have interpreted the short stories by South African writers in the book *Somehow Tenderness Survives,* compiled by Hazel Rochman. These art works are on exhibit in the library.

Apartheid "Found" Poetry Exhibit: Theresa Steinlage's creative writing class will prepare "found" poems about Apartheid in current articles. These are exhibited in the library.

Apartheid Book Exhibit: The Econo-Clad Book Company has provided a collection of books that are in the library display case.

Film Festival

Several outstanding films and videos concerning Apartheid are available in the library. If teachers choose to show one during Ethnic Week, contact the audio visual department, extension 81 in the Library.

Master Harold And The Boys	90 minutes
South Africa Belongs To Us	35 minutes
Cry Freedom	90 minutes
South Africa	30 minutes
Country Lovers	60 minutes
A Place For Weeping	60 minutes
The Last Grave At Dimbasa	60 minutes

An Interview with Sharon Krueger   50 minutes
   (foreign exchange student from South Africa)
South Africa   50 minutes
Apartheid Protest   10 minutes
   (held at the UN July 2, 1985)

Curriculum Projects

Students enrolled in composition classes with Mrs. Wilson will write informative papers based on ideas discussed in the book *Somehow Tenderness Survives,* compiled by Hazel Rochman. Mrs. Elmborg and Mr. Handley will team teach and discuss the same short stories to composition III and current event students during 1st hour. Mrs. Wardlow's international foods class will discuss the native foods of South Africa. In connection with the South African geography unit, Mr. Goehring's ninth grade social studies classes will discuss the short stories from *Somehow Tenderness Survives.*

Speaker's Bureau

Community leaders, Topeka Public School officials and members of Melanie Ralston's Forensics classes are prepared to inform Topeka West classes about Apartheid. If teachers wish to schedule speakers during the listed times, please schedule this activity with the Library secretary at extension 80.

Speaker	Available Time
Verlene Scroggins (South African Poetry)	Monday, March 6, 3rd hour
Curtis Hartenberger	Tuesday, March 7, 4th hour
Dr. Otudeko (Washburn University Anthropology Department)	Tuesday, March 7, 5th hour

Jonathan Leahey (Mark Harvey Washburn University Debaters)	Wednesday, March 8, 2nd hour
Sonny Scroggins	Wednesday, March 8, 3rd hour
Kay Meadows	Thursday, March 9, 1st hour
Nancy Hjetland	Thursday, March 9, 4-5 hours
Sherman Parks (Comparing U.S. in the 1960s to South Africa today)	Thursday, March 9, 5th hour
Dr. Gilbert Parks	Friday, March 10, 2nd hour
John Stumbo	Friday, March 10, 6th hour
Vanessa Harper (Forensics student, persuasive speech of "Country Lovers")	1st-2nd hour any day
Lorna Cable (Forensics student, oral interpretation of "The Road to Alexandra")	2nd hour any day

Somehow We Survive

By Dennis Brutus

Somehow we survive
and tenderness, frustrated, does not wither.

Investigating searchlights rake
our naked unprotected contours;

over our heads the monolithic decalogue
of fascist prohibition glowers
and teeters for a catastrophic fall;

boots club the peeling door.

But somehow we survive
severance, deprication, loss.

Patrols uncoil along the asphalt dark
hissing their menace to our lives,
most cruel, all our land is scarred with terror,
rendered unlovely; and unloveable;
murdered are we and all our passionate surrender

but somehow tenderness survives.

Source: *Somehow Tenderness Survives: Stories of Apartheid in Southern Africa* is compiled by Hazel Rochman and published by Harper and Row in 1988. This book has served as the basis for this week's activities.

HOLOCAUST

Lynda Miller, Charcoal

TOPEKA WEST HIGH SCHOOL LIBRARY

Presents

ETHNIC WEEK 1990

March 5-9, 1990

THE HOLOCAUST—NEVER TO BE FORGOTTEN

Purpose

To educate Topeka West students about the Holocaust, the library has scheduled several activities teachers and students may avail themselves of during the week of March 5-9, 1990. Classroom sets of the book *Auschwitz: True Tales of a Grotesque Land,* have been purchased. To schedule these books for classroom use, please call Diane at extension 80. There will be a display of Holocaust books, compliments of Econo-Clad Books, in the library during the week.

Library Forums

Library Forums will be held in the Library at the specified times. Please contact Mike Printz or Diane Goheen to schedule your class for these sessions.

Speaker   **Schedule Times**

Joe and Fela Igielnick   Wednesday, March 7, 3-4 hours
Ben Edelbaum
(Holocaust survivors)

Joe Zatzkis   Thursday, March 8, 8:30-10:00
(Former Army Intelligence Officer)

Yonat Klar   Tuesday, March 6, 2-3 hours
(One-Woman Show, CHILDHOOD)

Curriculum Projects

Students' work will be highlighted throughout the week. Original poetry written by Mr. Goheen's students in honors sophomore English will be displayed in the library. Students in Mrs. Ralston's forensics classes will be available to make classroom presentations during the week of March 5-9. To schedule a forensic presentation contact the library at ext. 80. Students in Mrs. Elmborg's and Mrs. Steinlage's composition classes will write original compositions on the Holocaust.

Speaker's Bureau

During the week, several speakers will be available to visit classes. Should you be interested in one of the following speakers and available times, please schedule these through Darlene Luellen at ext. 80

Speaker	Schedule
Rabbi Lawrence Karol (Anti-Semitism)	Monday, March 5, 3rd hour
Mr. Don Patterson (Dachau Liberator)	Monday, March 5, 4th hour
Dr. Gunter Alkninis (Washburn University Professor)	Tuesday, March 6, 5th hour
Dr. Lillian Kremer (Literature of the Holocaust Instructor)	Wednesday, March 7, 5th hour
Mrs. Mary Greenberg (Second Generation Survivor)	Friday, March 9, 1st hour
Dr. Herb Modlin (Psychiatrist at the Menninger Foundation)	Friday, March 9, 3rd hour
Ralph Rundquist	Friday, March 9, 4th hour

Film Festival

Playing for Time	2 hours 30 minutes
Julia	2 hours
The White Rose	1 hour 48 minutes
Kitty: A Return to Auschwitz	1 hour 22 minutes
Assissi Underground	1 hour 55 minutes
Sophie's Choice	2 hours 30 minutes
Nazi Germany: Years of Triumph	28 minutes
The Legacy: Children of the Holocaust	23 minutes
You Are Free	20 minutes
The Diary of Anne Frank	2 hours 30 minutes
Hitler: The Road to Revenge	30 minutes
The Pedestrian	1 hour 37 minutes
Hanna's War	1 hour 48 minutes
Partisans of Vilna	2 hours 10 minutes

The Boat is Full	1 hour 44 minutes
Revolt of Job	1 hour 37 minutes
Holocaust: In Dark Places	1 hour
Our Century: A Look at	
Jewish Survivors	1 hour 30 minutes
To Bear Witness	48 minutes
Shoah	9 hours 30 minutes

Additional Resources for Teachers

Mary Greenberg will serve as a resource person in preparation for this study. She would like to meet with teachers whose students will be participating in this study on Tuesday, February 20, from 3:00-4:00 P.M. in the Library Reference Room.

NATIVE AMERICAN

James Newman, Pen and Ink

TOPEKA WEST HIGH SCHOOL LIBRARY

PRESENTS

ETHNIC WEEK 1991

MARCH 4-8, 1991

WORDS IN THE BLOOD
AN AWARENESS OF NATIVE AMERICANS

Purpose

To educate Topeka West students about the Native American Experience, the library has scheduled several activities that teachers and students
may avail themselves of during the week of March 4-8, 1991. Classroom
sets of the book *Words in the Blood,* have been purchased. There will be
a display of Native American books and student work in the library during
the week.

Library Forums

Library forums will be held in the library at these specified times during Ethnic Week. Please contact Mike Printz or Diane Goheen to schedule your class.

Dallas Chief Eagle   Monday, March 4, 3-5 hours
   (Multi-media presentation)

Miss Haskell Dancers   Tuesday, March 5, 5th hour
   (Native American dance presentation)

Lucian McKinney   Wednesday, March 6, 2nd hour
   (presentation on Native American
   culture and language)

Pete Fee   Wednesday, March 6, 4th hour, 5th hour
   (presentation of the Native
   American as the Earth's caretaker)

Russell Blackbird   Thursday, March 7, 1st hour, 2nd hour
   (presentation on entwining the
   Native American culture and
   tradition into everyday life)

Jackson Lee   Thursday, March 7, 5th hour
   (presentation on reservation life
   and Native American religious
   beliefs and customs)

Native American Senior
Citizen/West Seniors Forum   Friday, March 8, 4th hour (11:15-12:15)

Speaker's Bureau

During the week, several speakers will be available to visit individual classes. Should you be interested in one of the following speakers and times, please schedule these through the library secretary, ext. 80.

George Wahquahboshkuk   Tuesday, March 5, 3rd hour
(Tribal Chairman Prairie Band Potowatomi)

Steve Cadue   Tuesday, March 5, 4th hour
(Tribal Chairman of the Kickapoo Nation)

Joseph Fast Horse   Thursday, March 7, 3rd hour
(Principal, Kickapoo Nation School)

Howard Allen   Thursday, March 7, 3rd hour
(Teacher, Kickapoo Nation School)

John Pearce   Thursday, March 7, 5th hour
(Chairman of the Judicial and
Legislative Committee for the
Shawnee County Allied Tribes)

Film Festival

These film titles will be available during Ethnic Week here in the
library. If you would like to schedule a film during this week, please
contact Kay at ext. 81.

American Indian Artists Series   3 at 60 minutes
Custer's Battlefield Archeological
  Survey of 1984   58 minutes
Pow Wow!   16 minutes
Sunflower Journey #209   29 minutes
Son of the Morning Star   2 hours
The American Indian Before the
  White Man Came   19 minutes
The American Indian After the
  White Man Came   27 minutes
American Indian Artists:
  Charles Loloma   20 minutes
Ancient Aztec Indians of
  North America   8 minutes
Broken Treaty at Battle Mountain   60 minutes
Children of the Long-Beaked Bird   29 minutes

Custer: The American Surge Westword	33 minutes
The Divided Trail: A Native American Odyssey	40 minutes
Haa Shagoon	29 minutes
Hopi: Songs of the Fourth World	61 minutes
Indian Artists of the Southwest	15 minutes
Indian Rights, Indian Law	30 minutes
The Loon's Necklace	11 minutes
Maria of the Pueblos	15 minutes
Red Sunday: The Story of the Battle of the Little Big Horn	28 minutes
Return to Sovereignty	46 minutes
Two Indians: Red Reflections of Life	26 minutes
Sentinels of Silence	19 minutes
Walking in a Sacred Manner	23 minutes
Billy Jack	1 hour 52 minutes
Tell Them Willie Boy Is Here	1 hour 38 minutes
War Party	1 hour 39 minutes
The White Dawn	1 hour 50 minutes
When The Legends Die	1 hour 45 minutes

Curriculum Projects

Student work will be highlighted throughout the week. Original poetry written by Mr. Goheen's students in honors sophomore English class will be displayed in the Library. Students in Mrs. Miller's, Mr. Fleming's, Mrs. Daniel's and Mr. Callaway's art classes will have variety of student work on display in the library. Library student coordinators for this Ethnic Week study are Steve Davis and Mike Kauffman.

Karli Pigg, Cut Paper

ETHNIC WEEK 1992

ASIAN-AMERICAN CULTURES

TOPEKA WEST HIGH SCHOOL

MARCH 2-6, 1992

Purpose

For this year's observance the library staff invites you to join us in raising our students' awareness concerning Asian-American cultures. One of these groups is the HMONG (pronounced Mung).

Brief History of the Hmong

The Hmong are people who began moving southward from northern China 5,000 years ago. They moved to the mountainous regions of Southeast Asia and many migrated to Laos. Sometimes they are referred to as "hill tribes" and sometimes they call themselves "free farmers." For years the Laotian-Hmong worked primarily as hunters and farmers. During the Vietnam War, however, many Hmong men and boys were recruited by the United States to serve as highly skilled jungle fighters. Because of this involvement in fighting, the Hmong were immediately forced out of Laos when the United States began pulling its forces out. Many Hmong fled across the Mekong River to Thailand refugee camps. From there, many have immigrated to new countries to begin new lives. Since 1976, approximately 100,000 have immigrated to various parts of the United States.

The Vietnam War, the migration to Thailand, and the more recent movement to the United States have caused great disruptions in the Hmong peoples' way of life. In Laos they had lived in relative isolation, but now they are being thrown into very complex modern living situations. Every aspect of their lives—their religious and medical practices, their language, their food customs, music and art—is undergoing some kind of change. Some of their traditions, such as wearing traditional clothes every day, will most likely have to be let go in their new country. Other customs, such as eating rice, they will be able to maintain.

As has happened before in their long history, the Hmong are being forced to adapt to strange situations, aided only by their resilience, stubbornness, independence and will to survive. Above all, the Hmong are survivors. They have not only salvaged and maintained much of their culture but have been generous in allowing other cultures to begin knowing them through their folk art and through their stories. Because their stories provide both unique and universal lessons that can be appreciated by all cultures, we have plans to bring Hmong storytellers to address our students.

One group of storytellers will be Hmong Boy Scouts. Thanks to Dr. McFrazier we have added multiple copies of the outstanding book *Dark Sky, Dark Land: Stories of the Hmong Boy Scouts of Troup 100*. Fifteen of the Scouts are featured in stories of escape from their homeland to freedom in the United States. The book also documents their stories of Hmong life in Laos during the Vietnam War, their escape to Thailand, arrival in the United States as refugees, and the adjustments to American society. Collectively, these stories reflect intense struggle, perseverance, love and ultimate victory.

On Wednesday, March 4, 1991 David L. Moore, Scoutmaster and author of *Dark Sky, Dark Land* and two of the Hmong Boy Scouts, Yee Chang and Chu Vue, will present library forums during hours 2, 3, 5, and 6. These forums are made possible by Dr. McFrazier and the Topeka West Booster Club.

If you wish to bring your classes to these forums and other library forums during Ethnic Week, your classes should read from the book complete other readings about the Hmong from a packet we have prepared and have three questions ready to ask our visitors. This kind of background preparation has allowed these forums to be successful in the past. If you are interested in participating, check with us as soon as possible to schedule a classroom set of books for your room. First-come, first-served. Because we anticipate many classes wishing to participate on March 4, make plans now to prepare.

TOPEKA WEST HIGH SCHOOL LIBRARY

PRESENTS

ETHNIC WEEK 1992

MARCH 2-5, 1992

BECAUSE I AM PART OF THE UNIVERSE, TOO
An Awareness of Asian-American Cultures

Purpose

The purpose of this year's Ethnic Week is to educate Topeka West Students about the Asian-American experience. The library has scheduled several activities for teachers and students during the week of March 2-6, 1992. Classroom sets of the book *Dark Sky, Dark Land* have been purchased. There will be a display of Hmong art, Asian books, and student work in the library during this week.

Library Forums

Library forums will be held in the library at the following specified times. Please contact Mike Printz or Diane Goheen to schedule your class for these events.

Monday, March 2:
    2nd hour   Martial Arts Demonstration
    3rd hour   Martial Arts Demonstration
    3rd hour   Cindy Lo, Chinese Garden
    6th hour   Chinese cooking demonstration

Tuesday, March 3:
    1st hour   John Carlin
    2nd hour   "The Role of Trade and Business in Asia"
    4th hour   Wim Chulindra, Thai "Second Generation Asians and the Successful Asian"
    5th hour   Ms. Elmborg's Composition
    6th hour   Composition III students will interview students from Fukuok University in Japan and produce written work from these interviews.

Wednesday, March 4:
    2nd hour   Hmong Boy Scout Troop 100 from Minneapolis, Minnesota
    3rd hour
    5th hour
    6th hour

Thursday, March 5:
    7:15 a.m.   Faculty Meeting (cafe) Hmong Boy Scout Troop 100
    1st hour   Hmong Boy Scout Troop 100
    3rd hour   Storytelling by Acting II students: John Lewis, Holly Harbaugh,

	Lauri Comstock, and Denise
	Akins (20 minute presentation)
4th hour	Dr. Sara Tucker University Professor
	"The Role of Women in Asian
	Cultures"

Friday, March 6:
    1st hour   Baili Chang, Washburn University
                                 MA student "China's Culture and
                                 Value Systems"
    2nd hour   Tanya Low
    3rd hour   Tanya Low, U.S.D. 501, teacher of
                                 Chinese "Early Asian-American
                                 Immigration to the United States"

Curriculum Projects

Student work will be highlighted throughout the week. Original prose and poetry by Mrs. Steinlage's classes will be on display in the Library. Art students will have various works on display in the library and A-building Hall. Mr. Goheen's acting II students will be available to make individual classroom presentations. (Please schedule these presentations through Diane Goheen.)

Bibliography

Lynda Miller

Allen, Paula Gunn. 1989. *Spider's Woman's Granddaughters: Traditional Tales and Contemporary Writing by Native American Women.* New York: Fawcett Columbine.

Armor, John and Peter Wright with photographs by Ansel Adams. 1988. *Manzanar.* New York: Times Books.

Banks, James A. "Multicultural Education: For Freedom's Sake," *Educational Leadership,* pp. 32-36. December 1991/January 1992.

Banks, James A. 1989. *Multicultural Education: Issues and Perspectives.* Needham Heights, MA: Allyn and Bacon.

Campbell, Joseph. 1976. *Creative Mythology: The Masks of God.* New York: Penguin Books.

Chan, Anthony and Norma J. Livo. 1990. *Hmong Textile Designs.* Baltimore, MD: Stemmer House Publishers.

Cooper, Charles R. and Lee Odell. 1977. *Evaluating Writing.* Urbana, IL: National Council of Teachers of English.

Debo, Angle. 1989. *A History of the Indians of the United States.* Norman, OK: University of Oklahoma Press.

Erdoes, Richard and Alfonso Ortiz. 1984. *American Indian Myths and Legends.* New York: Pantheon Press.

Gere, Anne Ruggles. 1985. *Roots in the Sawdust: Writing To Learn Across the Disciplines.* Urbana, IL: National Council of Teachers of English.

Godfrey, Robert. "Civilization, Education and the Visual Arts: A Personal Manifesto," pp. 596-600. *Phi Delta Kappan,* April, 1992.

Goheen, Diane and Mike Printz. "Sirens, Knuckles and Boots! Apartheid in South Africa," *Voya,* October, 1989.

Gordimer, Nadine. 1991. *Jump and Other Stories.* New York: Farrar, Straus, Giroux.

Grossman, Florence. 1982. *Getting From Here to There: Writing and Reading Poetry.* Montclair, NJ: Boynton/Cook Publishers, Inc.

Hamilton, Charles. 1989. *Cry of the Thunderbird: The American Indian's own Story.* Norman, OK: University of Oklahoma Press.

Highwater, Jamake. 1984. *Words in the Blood: Contemporary Indian Writers of North and South America.* New York: New American Library.

Kirby, Dan and Tom Liner with Ruth Vinz. 1988. *Inside Out: Developmental Strategies for Teaching Writing.* Portsmouth, NH: Boynton/Cook Publishers, Inc.

Lowry, Lois. 1989. *Number the Stars.* New York: Dell Publishing Co.

MacDowell, Marsh. 1988. *Hmong Folk Arts: A Guide for Teachers.* East Lansing, MI: Michigan State University Press.

MacDowell, Marsha. 1989. *Stories In Thread*. East Lansing, MI: Michigan State University Press.

Mathabane, Mark. 1986. *Kaffir Boy*. New York: A Plume Book, Penguin Books.

Mathabane, Mark. 1989. *Kaffir Boy in America*. New York: Collier Books, Macmillan Publishing.

Mittler, Gene A. 1986. *Art in Focus*. CA: Glencoe Publishing Company.

Moore, David L. 1989. *Dark Sky, Dark Land: Stories of the Hmong Boy Scouts of Troop 100*. Eden Prairie, MN: Tessera Publishing.

Nomberg-Przytyk, Sara. 1985. *Auschwitz: True Tales From A Grotesque Land*. Chapel Hill, NC: The University of North Carolina Press.

Padgett, Ron. 1987. *Handbook of Poetic Forms*. New York: The Teachers and Writers Collaborative.

Ramsey, Patricia G. 1987. *Teaching and Learning in a Diverse World: Multicultural Eduction for Young Children*. New York: Teachers College, Columbia University.

Rochman, Hazel. 1992. *Against Borders: Promoting Books for a Multicultural World*. Chicago: Booklist/American Library Association.

Rochman, Hazel. 1988. *Somehow Tenderness Survives: Stories of Southern Africa*. New York: Harper Collins.

Rosenberg, Donna. 1988. *World Mythology: An Anthology of the Great Myths and Epics*. Lincolnwood, IL: National Textbook Company.

Roukes, Nicholas. 1988. *Design Synectics: Stimulating Creativity in Design*. Worchester, MA: Davis Publications.

Silko, Leslie Marmon SIlko. 1981. *Storyteller*. New York: Arcade Publishing, Little, Brown and Company.

Sleeter, Christine E. 1991. *Empowerment Through Multicultural Education*. Albany, NY: State University of New York Press.

Troyna, Barry and Bruce Carrington. 1990. *Education, Racism and Reform*. New York: Routledge.

Williams, Robert L. 1977. *Cross-Cultural Education: Teaching Toward a Planetary Perspective*. Washington, DC: National Education Association.

Index